CW01425762

The Book of FIRE: Financial Independence Retire Early

Research: James Miller, Helen Sykes, Peter Guthridge, Mark Gregory and Shawn Willis

Written by the some of the world's greatest finance experts.

Edited By Kizzi Nkwocha (c)

A revision of Financial Freedom: Thought Leaders Edition originally published in November 2016.

This fifth edition is published with pride by Athena Publishing and Mithra Publishing 2019

www.athenapublishing.com

www.mithrapublishing.com

THE BOOK OF FIRE: FINANCIAL INDEPENDENCE RETIRE EARLY

"Your time is limited, so don't waste it living someone else's life. Don't be trapped by dogma – which is living with the results of other people's thinking. Don't let the noise of other's opinions drown out your own inner voice. And most important, have the courage to follow your heart and intuition. They somehow already know what you truly want to become. Everything else is secondary."

Steve Jobs

"My definition of financial freedom is simple: it is the ability to live the lifestyle you desire without having to work or rely on anyone else for money."

T. Harv Eker

Contributors to this book:

Justin McMillan, Andrew Pennie, Lowell G. Miller, Andrew Neligan, Paul Mahoney, Aoife Gaffney, Fanny Snaith, Jan Watman, Michelle Hutchison, Brett Jones, Ruth Warlow, Dave Nelson, Colin Lawson, Craig Richards, Chris Gray, Amanda Cassar, Peter Locandro and Clayton Daniel.

Inside THE BOOK OF FIRE

Introduction   14

About Kizzi Nkwocha   17

Why Financial Freedom is Important   19

How To Become Financially Free By Investing   30

Financial Freedom and Retirement   44

The Secrets Of A Successful Retirement   62

The Benefits of Peer-to-Peer Lending   74

Buy to Let Property   90

Understanding Your Relationship with Money   106

100 Tips for Saving Money and Getting Financially Fit   119

How To Pay Off Your Mortgage 10 Years Sooner   135

Go First Class, Go Commercial   146

Financial Freedom And Network Marketing   153

Network Marketing and Financial Freedom In Two To Four Years   163

Taxing Times   172

The Mindset Of A Successful Investor   182

Property Investment Is Your Ticket To Freedom   191

The Ten Commandments Of Property Investing   195

Why You're Better Off Ringside – The Perils Of Going It Alone In Property
                                                            198

Positive Income Generators   200

How Long Is A Piece Of String? Creating Wealth For Your Retirement   219

Avoiding Fears Is Stronger Than Achieving Goals   228

Introduction

Financial freedom comes easiest to those who understand that it is a state of mind as much as a state of being.

Despite our many accomplishments in life and in business, acquiring financial freedom is truly one of the biggest achievements that you should strive for in your life.

Having said this, acquiring financial freedom is not an instant process; it is rather a gradual and step by step process with the end result being that you have Financial Freedom with you.

That's where this book becomes an invaluable resource.

Over the course of a year and four months we have drawn on the collective wisdom of acclaimed experts from every aspect of personal finance to help put this book together. The one common theme you will find running through this book like a golden thread is the belief that financial freedom encompasses many other aspects such as a happy family life, good bank balance, living a debt free and risk free life and the capacity to full fill your cherished dreams and desires of your life. Financial freedom puts you in control of your money rather than money controlling your life. Financial freedom gives you the power to live life according to your own terms. It is the real victory and one of the greatest achievements of your life.

The glaring reality is that the only way to overcome money problems is to start taking matters into your own hands. You must become proactive and take some immediate remedial action. Let our experts guide you along this path.

I sincerely believe that you cannot change your financial past but you can change your financial future. Constructive change will only result when you decide to take control of your circumstances. You have taken the first step towards that new future by reading The Book of FIRE: Financial Independence Retire Early.

"Money is like a sixth sense without which you cannot make a complete use of the other five."

Kizzi Nkwocha

About Kizzi Nkwocha

Kizzi Nkwocha is a public speaker and the publisher of Money and Finance Magazine, Business Game Changer Magazine, The UK Newspaper, The Property Investor and The Sussex Newspaper. He is the chairman of The Ethical Publishers Association (ETHPA).

Kizzi Nkwocha made his mark in the UK as a publicist, journalist and social media pioneer. As a widely respected and successful media consultant Nkwocha has represented a diverse range of clients including the King of Uganda, mistresses of President Clinton, Amnesty International, Pakistani cricket captain Wasim Akram, campaign group Jubilee 2000, Dragons Den businessman, Levi Roots and world record teenage sailor, Michael Perham.

Nkwocha has also become a well-known personality on both radio and television. He has been the focus of a Channel 4 documentary on publicity and has hosted his own talk show, London Line, on Sky TV.

He also co-presented a weekly current affairs program in Spain on Radio Onda Cero International and both radio and TV shows in Cyprus.

His books have included the fiction novel, *Heavens Fire*, the business guide books: Business, Business, Business!, Mind Your Own Business, Insiders Know-How: Public Relations and the international bestseller SocMed: Social Media For Business. His second fiction book, *Donald Bryan And The Prophecy Of The Popes*, is due out in November 2019. In 2011 his team won the SIPA award for social media.

Follow Kizzi on Twitter: https://twitter.com/kizzinkwocha
Listen to his business podcast at:
https://podcasts.apple.com/fr/podcast/kizzis-friday-game-changers/id1475230711?l=en&ls=1

Why Financial Freedom is Important

In my 15 years as a financial adviser, advising and assisting hundreds of clients, I have never had a client say they do not want financial freedom. However, when I ask clients what financial freedom means to them, very few can articulate what it looks like.

How does this happen? How do so many of us get up every morning and go off to work with the ultimate aim of being financial free, but we do not actually know what it looks like? And if we do not know what it looks like it is almost certain that it will not be achieved, because:

> ➤ If you are not crystal clear on what financial freedom means for you, i.e. you do not know what it looks like – what you will be doing, with whom and where etc., how can you calculate how much money you are going to need to fund your financial freedom?
> ➤ If you do not how much your financial freedom is going to cost, how do you calculate the level of wealth you are going to need to accumulate?
> ➤ If you do not know the level of wealth you need to accumulate, how do you know how much you are going to need to save?

What is Your Life Purpose?

So, before you start studying strategies, investment and options, the above questions need to be answered. It is like going to a car yard and asking for a new car to take on holidays and the car sales person replies with a number of questions; how long are you going on holidays? Are you going to be towing a caravan? Will you be going off road? Until these questions are answered the sales person will not be able to recommend options. Another example would be like going to see a personal trainer and asking for help and, once again, they are going to reply with a number of questions ; Are you looking to lose weight? Build your muscles? Lean up or train for a marathon? Each of these options is going to require different training. This is exactly the same when it comes to money and planning for the future. We all have unique aspirations and, therefore, we are all going to have unique paths to financial freedom.

The following outlines the process to follow to gain crystal clarity on what financial freedom means to you.

Step 1: What You Want to Do More and Less of?

Take time and reflect on if the amount you see as financial freedom, e.g. $5 million, $10 million etc., landed in your bank tomorrow, you could create a list all the things you would do more of, all the things you would no longer do and what would you do less of.

Step 2: Re-Connect With Your Life Purpose

While reflecting, take the time to connect with what you see as your life purpose. The best way (though a bit morbid) to make this connection is to imagine you are at your own funeral. What do you hope people will say about you? If you passed away today would people actually say this about you?

Step 3: Your Fundamental Requirements

List what your fundamental requirements are and will be in the future. For example, what are your minimum requirements for comfortability?

These include necessities:

- ➤ Housing
- ➤ Rates
- ➤ Food
- ➤ Power
- ➤ Water

And discretionary spending (which you will not forgo under any circumstances, because they are important to you)

- ➢ Housing maintenance
- ➢ Health
- ➢ Children's education and activities
- ➢ Car and transport
- ➢ Entertainment
- ➢ Fitness
- ➢ Personal care
- ➢ Clothing

Once you have your list:

- ➢ Set up a spreadsheet.
- ➢ Download your bank/credit card statement.
- ➢ Enter the average amounts from your bank/credit card into your spreadsheet. Do not estimate, use the actual amounts, because if you estimate the amounts you will always underestimate.
- ➢ Total up the amounts either on a weekly, monthly or yearly basis.
- ➢ Total the expenses together and convert to an annual amount.
- ➢ Build in a 20% buffer as an emergency allocation.

Step 4: Your Aspirations

(On completion of Step 1) List all of your unmet aspirations in thorough detail. These unmet aspirations could include:

- ➢ Travel – when I suggest listing 'in thorough detail' I do not mean go on more holidays, I mean document where your ideal holiday would be, who you are going to go with, where you are going to stay, how long you are going to stay etc.
- ➢ Charity work – document who you are going to help and how.
- ➢ Starting your own business – what is your business going to look like? Who is your target market? How you are going to solve the problems for your target market and add value to their lives?
- ➢ Rediscovering your passion – go back in time to a time when the world was your oyster (before life started to get in the way). What was your passion? If it is still your passion, detail every aspect of it.

> ➢ Work less – detail what you want to do instead – what would you be doing? Where would you be spending your time? Who would you be spending your time with?

Step 5: Aspirations with Meaning

Once you have listed all of your aspirations, highlight those which have personal significance/meaning for you and document why they are significant to you. Also include how you would feel, or what it would mean to you, when you experience your aspiration.

Step 6: Your Top 5

Once you have a list of aspirations which have personal significance to you then short-list them down to your top five.

Step 7: Date Night

(For those who are a couple) it's time to bring your individual top 5 aspirations together and rank them as a couple. There is no better way to do this than having a date night and exploring each other's aspirations over a nice bottle of wine and/or a delicious meal.

Step 8: Vision Board

Now (as an individual or as a couple) you have crystal clarity on what your ideal future looks like. It is time to document in a manner that is going to keep you motivated. For most people this is in the form of a vision board. To do this get a large piece of cardboard, then Google for images that represent your aspirations. Fasten these images to the board and then secure the board to an area which you are going to see every day, i.e. your fridge, office etc. This will allow your subconscious to start to modify your behavior similar to the impact of finding a picture of your ideal body image and placing it on the fridge as your motivation when trying to lose weight/get fitter.

The Pathway to Financial Freedom

Now you have crystal clarity on where you want to be you can start working on how to get there.

Step 1: Get an Understanding of Where You Are At

Before you set off on your path to where you want to be, you need an understanding of where you are at – i.e, you need to get a thorough understanding of your numbers with an honest assessment. The only way to get this honest assessment is to go to the source of truth – your bank statements. Therefore, print out your bank statements for the last 12 months and categorise each transaction into areas and then document your expenses per category into a spreadsheet (yes I know another spreadsheet, but this spreadsheet will change your life) and total up each category for the year. Be prepared to be shocked at how much you spend in particular areas, people always are. This is a good thing. It means you have a starting point to work from.

Once you have recovered from the shock of how much you spend go through each category and ask yourself one question: Does this spending fall into one of the following three areas?

1) Is it a necessity? And pay television, a gym membership or Netflix is not a necessity.
2) Is it discretionary spending that helps define who I am? E.g., going to the gym everyday helps with my physical, mental and emotional health.
3) Is it spending/investing that is helping me get closer to where I want to be?

If the item does not fall into any one of these areas then stop spending, close down the direct debits for it, cancel the subscriptions, do what you have to do to stop allocating funds to this area.

Step 2: Confront Your Money Fears

For a significant percentage of people, their history with money has left them fearful of money and therefore is holding them back from achieving financial freedom. This will always hold them back until these fears are confronted and overcome. These are some of the fears I have encountered regularly and how the client overcame them:

> - "Money stresses me so once I get it I just have to spend it, so I can get rid of the stress" – I helped the client set up separate accounts for different purposes along with automatic direct debits, so when the client received money it was instantly transferred so only their spending money was left in their account.
> - "I am no good with numbers" – Seek advice from someone you trust who can explain the complex, simply so they can educate you over time.
> - "I have made bad money decisions in the past and do not trust myself" – Everybody makes bad money decisions as no one can predict the future. Even the world's most famous investor Warren Buffett gets it wrong about 30% of the time.

Step 3: Negotiate

Set aside one day a year (you will probably save more on this one day than you earn any other day during the year) to go through your bank statement and call all of your service providers (e.g. bank, electricity provider, water provider, internet provider, phone provider etc.) and tell them that you will be calling two other alternate providers. But before you call them you are giving them the opportunity to see what they can do. Then call two alternate providers and compare what is on offer.

Step 4: Get Advice on What is Possible and What is Required

Ask people you trust who they seek financial advice from and, based on their recommendations, seek financial modelling advice on which of the items on your vision board are possible and how much you need to save to achieve these. Following this process delete from your vision board the items which are not achievable or you are unwilling to save for (because if this is the case, then, in reality, they are not that important to you).

Step 5: Get Advice on How to Get There

Now you have crystal clarity on:

- ➤ Where you are.
- ➤ Where you want to be and know that where you want to be is possible.
- ➤ The level of savings required and you are committed to these level of savings.

It is time to get advice on the best strategy to achieve each of your aspirations as follows including: why it is the best strategy, other options, the implications of the best strategy, inbuilt potential flexibility (for changes in markets, legislation, your circumstances and your aspirations). Also the modelling should include the target benchmarks you need to achieve each year to ensure you remain on track.

Step 6: Track Your Progress

Just because you now have your documented pathway to financial freedom, it is simply not going to just happen, it needs attention, but do not worry if it is not day in, day out. You should sit down every 6 months, any shorter and you will be caught up in too much 'money noise' and any longer and you may drift off course.

The following should be included in your tracking analysis (either with your adviser or your self-assessment):

- ➤ Are you in front or behind of your target benchmarks?
- ➤ If you are behind, is it because of the performance of your investments or has the strategy not worked as anticipated?
- ➤ If you are behind because of the performance of your investment is it because markets are going through a flat or downward period (which all markets go through)? Or is it because the actual investment is underperforming their index? If it is the latter, contact the investment manager and interrogate them about their

performance. Based on their answers either elect to stay or move (remember to take tax implications into consideration).

➤ If it is the strategy then go back to the original options and once again compare.

The Theory in Practice

So how should this be implemented in practical terms? Let's examine David and Melissa, who I recently assisted through this process. David and Melissa are in their late 30s, have (what most people would see as) good jobs – David is a lawyer and Melissa is a part-time English teacher. David and Melissa have three children. Though they see themselves as financially literate they were starting to question if they were on the right path or if they should be doing more with their money.

When I met with David and Melissa they partially owned their home, which was nearly 20 years old. Though a good size, the floor plan was starting to become a challenge for them. By constantly making additional repayments, their mortgage sat at 400,000. They enjoyed taking their kids up the coast for their annual camping holiday and also managed to get over to the UK to see Melissa's parents about every two years. As well as their home they also owned an apartment in the city, which was being funded by the rent. So on the face of it they were doing plenty of sound things, but they still had doubts.

The meeting started by my asking Melissa what she fundamentally wanted their money to provide. After a few minutes of silence, Melissa confirmed she was struggling with the question, answering with the common default response of "for my family to be comfortable". I rephrased the question for her: "No matter what I say today what areas do you still want your money to fund?" This resonated with her and out poured the answers. "I want to still go camping with the family as we need that quality time with each other as we are so busy week to week. I want the kids to go to a private school, I want David and I to have our monthly date night, I want to keep healthy and go to the gym." Melissa continued for another five minutes.

I then asked her to take a leap of faith and assume for the next 20 minutes that, if we worked together, we could fund all of these fundamentals. "Beyond the fundamentals you have described what are your unmet aspirations, and in particular the ones which have personal significance to you?" Melissa, hesitantly said: "I would like to start my own home business." I asked her why this was significant to her. She replied: "To be an inspiration to my children. I also want to be able to send my daughters to university, as I grew up in the country and did not have the opportunity. I also want to be able to compete in the Australian Triathlon Champions, it is my personal challenge, so I would love to have the money for that."

It was then David's turn to be put under the spotlight. David agreed with Melissa that continuing to go camping with their family was a must. He also said his passion for motorbikes was non-negotiable, so they will need to replace his motorbike every 5 years.

David outlined that he wanted to have his own practice within 10 years, which specializes in pro-bono work for migrants. As the son of migrant parents, David saw his parents struggle. He said: "helping people like my parents is my purpose." Knowing the work that is going to be involved, David said he wanted a gap year to go on a road trip with his family.

We then prioritised the above in line with the following:

1. University for children.
2. David his own business & gap year 10 years – have their mortgage paid off before this can happen.
3. Melissa her own business – start now, benchmark on ongoing basis and slowly build up to do it in 10 years.

From here we developed their vision board, which now sits with pride on their fridge.

I then modelled if all of these were possible, which they were. However, David and Melissa needed to agree the following savings, which meant going without their comfort money, i.e. always having money in their pocket to buy things as it took their fancy, **but they knew that comfort money was not going to make them happy, living their life purposes would**:

- ➤ Savings for university - $11,000 a year.
- ➤ Pay off their mortgage in 10 years (to allow both David and Melissa start their own businesses, which they believe are their life purposes– additional mortgage repayments of $12,500 a year.

I am now in the process of putting together their target benchmark, examining appropriate strategies and investments. David and Melissa have committed to a 6 monthly check in program. David and Melissa understand commitment is required, but they see forgoing a night of TV once every 6 months to analyse their finances is a minor inconvenience compared to having the assurance and confidence in knowing that they are on the pathway to their future ideal life.

Financial freedom is achievable; I have provided you with the blueprint. It is now for you to choose if you want it or not!

Justin McMillan

About the author

Justin had 15 years of experience in providing financial advice and money coaching to 100s of clients. Currently, Justin is Director and Principal Adviser at Smartwealth.

At Smartwealth we are different to the majority of financial planning firms, whose focus is to sell you financial products. We get the most enjoyment in listening to clients passionately articulate what they most value and their dreams. Dreams we all have, but are often lost during the day-to-day treadmill of life. For us, there is nothing more satisfying than continually meeting with our clients, going through the wealth they are building, but more importantly listening to their increased passion for life on the back of their improved financial position, which allows them to spend more quality time with loved ones as well as pursuing their passions.

In essence, we do what do to empower our highly valued clients to live their life purposes.

How To Become Financially Free By Investing

The investment world today is awash in a surfeit of information. There is a continuous, unstoppable river of facts. It can get overwhelming, prompting some to give up the quest for outstanding investments in individual companies, and opt instead for an index or a sub-index, accepting the "bad" companies in the group to which they've "allocated" along with the good companies in whose prosperity they seek to participate. Fund flows that equally buy the best and the worst stocks (and everything in between) in an index magnify the trend, and computer programs run by large organizations with no thought to business fundamentals or prospects exacerbate, for now, the homogeneous performance of stocks and high correlations of return that appear to ignore the true differences between companies. Like any investment fad, this looks like an easy path and it works—until it doesn't.

But does it work? Allocation instead of analysis and investment fits well into a spreadsheet, but how it fits into the real world is another question. There is really no significant edge in allocating to size or style, though it may seem so in a myopic time frame.

Observe in this table that if you "chose" style or size—over the past 5 and 10 years, at least—you might have rolled the dice correctly in a one-year horizon, but the further out in time you go, the less return advantage there has been in selecting any category over another. Indeed, all the returns converge. As time unfolds, there is not enough difference in style and size returns to make a difference!

We've often had team discussions about how we can add value in a world where categories—such as domestic, small value, large growth, large value, or the many industry sectors—ultimately converge. We always reach the same conclusion: investing by allocation isn't really investing; it's a kind of spreadsheet exercise dedicated to diversification, but divorced from the real world of businesses and how they succeed or fail.

The facts of today are known by all, and to that extent the market is roughly efficient. But true investing, as opposed to allocation, should involve having vision, seeing around corners, understanding the most likely scenario for a company's future, envisioning some possible alternative scenarios, identifying the probabilities of each becoming reality, and knowing the risks if the narrative fails.

For many, it is an uncomfortable thought to be at the mercy of impending unknowns—especially when the subject is money. But if you begin with a solid foundation of quality companies, "good news" can make them better than they were, and lift them into the "good" constituents of an index, above the "bad."

Atop the basics of sound finances, a reliable market for a company's goods and services, proven management, shareholder appreciation (think dividends), and industry conditions that are amenable to success, here are four kinds of "good news" tailwinds we try to position ourselves in front of:

1. **High and rising dividends.** This is fundamental to our approach in most of our strategies. We believe that dividends themselves are representative of a company that is mature and strong enough to pay them. All else being equal, we view these stocks as having lower risk compared to the broad market. Among other qualities, we believe dividends confirm a company's previous financial reporting, since the company has to pay them in cash. Dividend *increases,* in our opinion, are a message from management that the future will be something like the past, but better. And rising dividends can ultimately have the same effect on a stock price that rising rents can have on the value of rental real estate—they make

the asset more valuable. Assuming purchase at a reasonable price, the "good news" that we hope for in this kind of stock, apart from any other developments, are dividend increases equal to or in excess of our expectations, and above comparable companies.

2. **Cheapness.** Let's face it, the markets in general and individual stocks in particular are only partly priced on facts. After all, the prices are changing constantly, even when the facts are not. Just consider, most recently, the "model" behavior of investors around the financial crisis of 2008. Whether it had to do with secular positioning (through derivatives) or not, the only way to interpret stock prices in the fall of 2008 was that they expressed a view that the world was coming to an end. To be sure, events within the financial system provoked doubts about the overall economy and all the companies within it, but scores of important American businesses dropped to single-digit prices and PE ratios, even companies with little or no debt and solid recurring market demand for their products and services. All you had to do to get in the way of good news back then was to assert that no, the world was not coming to an end. Not a bad bet. One could not know the exact outcome or timing, but one could know that consumers will not stop eating, or using electricity or phones, buying soap, or for that matter, banking in their local banks.

This kind of event may be rare in the markets or the economy, but it seems to happen to individual stocks all the time. For example, investors get a notion that hard disk drives are dead because fewer PCs are being sold, so they dump the hard drive makers. But they forget that more than 90% of the world's data has been created in the past few years, and it all needs to be stored. Where? On server farms, whose storage needs are met by the hard drive makers. Furthermore, drives, it is claimed, are being displaced everywhere by solid-state memory. Who are the makers of solid-state memory? A few newbies in the field, but also in a major way the market is owned by the hard drive makers. So the world was not ending for these companies, though investors acted that way, and afterward, there was an opportunity to buy them at single-digit PE ratios and yields higher than junk bonds—with balance sheets that were rock-solid.

3. **Economic inevitability.** In the late 1990s we came to understand, through our expertise in the utilities sector, that there would be massive consolidation among utilities in the aftermath of the repeal of PUHCA (the Public Utility Holding Company Act), which in effect had prohibited most utility mergers. The act was originally passed to break up pyramidal national utility holding companies such as those created by Samuel Insull, who saw that the only thing better than having a monopoly on an essential service was having an even bigger monopoly. Why this insight would have escaped the notice of contemporary utilities was not apparent, and indeed when the opportunity to grow through acquisition presented itself, they didn't shy away from it. Given these observations, we bought, in our specialty strategy dedicated to the M&A heaven we envisioned, stocks with high and rising dividends that we would be happy to own even if they were not acquired. Most were, but the point is that our downside was covered by owning quality companies in a proven industry even as we sought the upside of merger transactions.

Today there are a number of industries where economic inevitability colors their future: newspapers, books, broadcast television, wire-line voice telecom, and maybe combustion engine parts makers before long.

Who will want them is far from obvious to us, yet if the valuation of individual companies is cheapened enough by emotional sellers, they can offer a kind of economic inevitability in their appeal for strategic buyers. And financial (private equity) buyers, whose agenda is to make money regardless of the business, always lurk when investors in the secondary market sell down a stock to bargain levels.

4. **Time frame and turnarounds.** There are exceptions, but most gains and losses can be sudden. Yet most investors seem to have a patience threshold that inhibits them from holding sleepers. They want stocks performing all the time, 24/7. When a company encounters problems, whether it be from changes in its end-user marketplace, management difficulties, overleveraging, commodity price changes, or the simple failure of a product or initiative, investors lose enthusiasm (a milder form of the "model" noted in #2) and lose faith. A 20 PE stock becomes a 10 PE stock due to reduced growth expectations—even if earnings and dividends hold up—and as traders like to say, it just sits there as attention shifts to other companies.

To be sure, there are companies that lose their mojo, or prove to be either one-hit wonders or "smart" at a given point in time but not so smart when conditions change for them. But as Jeff Vinik, former portfolio manager of Magellan Fund, said when he was first appointed, "the big money is in turnarounds." The question becomes one of the staying power of a company, and what it can do to return to former levels of profitability. Our job as managers becomes one of constructing a reasonable scenario, and understanding that it may take time.

By accepting the frequent need for patience in a potential turnaround, you avoid the "next quarter" mentality of an index-chasing strategy, and don't have to worry whether or not a stock is leading the index today.

Change happens in bits and pieces, but when investors finally do embrace a change from troubled future to incipient happy days, there is a tipping point, and price moves can be short and sharp. Positioning for this possible good news means developing confidence that the floor is somewhere near, and that the bog of a "value trap" is not.

In other words, would a stock fit within our portfolio at more modest expectations even if a turnaround doesn't develop?

Conclusion:

So these are four moments of positioning in the way of good news that enhance the standard mandatory requirements for quality, durability, income (where appropriate), and normal growth expectations. We've often called these aspects the "story of the stock." Others have called them "growth kickers" or "catalysts," though in all cases there may be an element of sentiment analysis and business-politics evaluation that go beyond those standard terms. The real point is how to add value in a world in which the facts are widely known, and even the thresholds by which the facts are judged to be positive or negative are widely known. One must develop a narrative—and as far as we know no spreadsheet has ever spontaneously suggested a future that's different from the present.

In the best of all possible worlds, a stock will have it all—solid financials, high and rising income for investors, a durable business, cheapness (based on its own history and/or relative to the current market metrics) driven down by negative sentiment, a likely fit with another company, and good chances for internal improvement. It is not often that all these factors occur in one company, but that is our quest, nevertheless. And the overall portfolio can represent all these factors among different stocks, if the portfolio itself is seen as a kind of ideal stock.

With the indices at historically high valuations and interest rates likely having seen a bottom, individual stocks are a more likely source of returns than the "unwashed" market in coming years. We've outlined above our approach, which despite all the changes in the world around us, has not changed conceptually since 1991 when we first began active management. It's all about avoiding the noise of the stock marketplace with that single question: Would you want to own the whole company at this price? Then all that we've discussed enters in: reported numbers, comparisons to others, sentiment of investors, chances for a single buyer at a premium, rising income, opportunities for improvement or turn-around, the simple possibility of continued present success, and of course, a reasonable price.

In the spirit of avoiding the noise – lessons from the field of behavioral finance. Over the past two decades both investors and academicians have studied the human side of investing—as opposed to the balance sheets and income statements of accountancy. Known as behavioral finance, this discipline looks at how the mind and emotions play a role in our investing decisions. Investor weaknesses and mental errors are problems that drive down returns and appear to be universal among all people.

Only two things can be responsible for poor investment outcomes: future events that unfold in unanticipated ways, or investment errors that are a result of misperception, denial, incomplete evaluation, or yes, greed and fear. We all believe we're making rational decisions, but behavioral finance tells a different story.

It isn't just the investment vehicle that goes from point A to point B. It's you, the driver. In the 1990s, Dalbar conducted a now-famous study called Quantitative Analysis of Investor Behavior (QAIB). It studied the difference between fund re- turns and what investors actually got after moving in and out of their funds. It found that 5-year returns for the average growth fund during the period ending December 31, 1995, were 12%. But average investor returns were only 2.5%. Why the difference? The fund may have been fine, but most investors, apparently, were buying at the tops and selling at the lows. Assets flowed into the funds after they'd had great years and their "track record" appealed to the investors' greed—prompting "the crowd" to jump aboard the shiny train. But then assets flowed right back out when the previous pace could not be sustained. Ironically, "average" investors were most comfortable investing when the funds were highest, and least comfortable investing when the funds were cheapest.

Meantime, the most recent QAIB 2017, which looks at actual investor returns in equity, fixed-income, and asset allocation funds over the past 30-year period to December 30, 2016, concluded that very little about investor behavior has changed. Investors continue to be their own worst enemy, sabotaging returns by buying high, selling low, trying to "time" the market, and lacking patience to sustain a long-term vision. The study found that the average investor stayed in- vested for only four years, earning less—and in many cases a lot less—than if they had just patiently held on to their investments. Looking at any number of rolling 10-year periods, it does not appear that investors receive more than half the returns of mutual funds. Not insignificantly, Dalbar's 30-year time span encompasses the 1987 crash, the tech bubble and terrorism crash, the crash of 2008, and the recovery leading up to the most recent bull market.

The pressing problem for all of us is that the human brain and emotions are poorly adapted to the investing environment. It's a kind of biological design flaw, exacerbated by the ultimately unknowable nature of the future. Academic scholars and students of behavioral finance have made a huge effort to discover the specific elements of our internal systems that fail in the face of market activities, and have articulated a good many categories or moments of behavioral finance that an investor can use to look deep inside him or her- self as a kind of GPS for what most often goes wrong in the process. Actual clinical studies and commentary from leading thinkers and researchers such as Thaler, Kahneman, Shiller, Statman, Tversky, Lakonishok, and others—the first three, Nobel Prize winners for their work—have much to tell us. The hard part is realizing that it is us they are talking about, not some "other" person making questionable decisions.

Bear in mind that the markets are not—as has often been postulated—made up of rational actors making fully informed decisions. Investors are actually human beings filled with hopes and dreams and fear and con- fusion. In other words, investors exhibit all the human frailties found in every other realm of living. Character traits don't magically dissolve away the moment a person begins to act as an investor. That would be like saying one can change completely just by moving to another city. We need to become aware of these traits in ourselves in order to understand them—and hope- fully, change our investing behavior.

4 PILLARS OF BEHAVIORAL FINANCE

Investors who grasp the link between their own psychology and the economic decisions that influence their financial well-being will gain insights that may help them in other areas of life besides their personal finances. Behavioral finance has identified four main concepts that describe why investors get into trouble with their decision making.

PILLAR #1. Our emotions around loss are strong. University of Chicago professor Richard Thaler showed that in clinical settings people feel the negative emotional force of a loss more than two times stronger than they feel the positive emotional force of a gain. A loss makes us feel like losers. It makes us "recognize" we were wrong—when we've spent all our lives trying to be right. A loss makes us feel like a victim, vulnerable to the threats of the world. If our advisor takes a loss, suddenly that guy who seemed so smart is now maybe an ignorant idiot. So we do everything we can—often unconsciously—to avoid all those negative feelings. Behavioral finance theorists call this "loss aversion."

PILLAR #2. Our mind makes pictures of bad out- comes. This is loss aversion's bully cousin, which the academics call prospective regret. Moved by prospective regret, a holder of a big gain begins to worry: If I don't sell now and it begins to fall, will I have lost the profits I would have "earned"? What if I sell now and the stock keeps going higher? I'll feel like a scaredy-cat idiot. What if earnings are bad? What if earnings are good? What if the Chinese do something? What if Trump posts a tweet? The last thing we want to tell ourselves is "I would've or I could've or I should've," so we take an action to escape the stress of our perseverating prospective regret.

Same with selling. We don't want to take a loss, for all that it symbolizes. Prospective regret comes to the rescue, suggesting—nay, insinuating—to the mind that the stock has already gone down enough and it's due for a rebound. The loss-averting mind likes to hear that; it means it doesn't have to decide to sell. And thus the circle is complete: The discomfort and pain of loss is affirmed and supported by prospective regret. Profits not taken, losses not booked. What hope is there for a human mind to buy low and sell high?

Meir Statman, a key figure in the field and professor of finance at Santa Clara University, puts it this way: "Loss aversion prompts investors to sell winning stocks too early. The pain of regret is more powerful than greed. Investors with winning positions sell early in order to avoid the imagined regret they will have if they fail to realize the profits they currently have. And it works in reverse. Losing positions are held all the way to disaster, in hopes of avoiding the certification of a loss, as the loss is just an abstraction until taken."

PILLAR #3. Our self-control switch is broken. We're not nearly as in control of ourselves as often or deeply as we think. We are, in many respects, a bundle of habits held inside a bag of skin with a proper name on it. As Thaler noted, in life we eat too much, we don't exercise enough, we have a terrible time kicking old habits, and our decisions are often driven by emotions. Yet we're very good at suppressing that fact. Could our inability to halt self-destructive behaviors be why investors have so much trouble investing in a disciplined way?

PILLAR #4. "Overconfidence" skews our decisions. Investors love to have opinions and imagine they have a gift for seeing into the future. Thus the world of the market becomes a debate contest in which everyone has an opinion and is fairly certain of its correctness. People learn to imitate each other, so when one loud- mouth on TV presents with great surety a picture of what will happen, investors, either overtly or within their small inner voices, follow suit.

They strongly "believe" that this stock will beat or this stock will swoon. But isn't that behavior rather maladapted to a world in which the future is essentially unknown? We don't know what will happen; we don't "know" if earnings will beat or miss, we don't know what a company's management is planning. As New Age gurus like to say: "We don't know what we don't know." If we can really digest this truth, it will ward off the dangers of overconfidence.

PREVENTING INVESTOR BEHAVIOR MISTAKES

There are many more principles and concepts of behavioral finance, but we've provided a healthy dose to get you started on the path to investor self-awareness. Self-awareness is essential if one wants to avoid in- vesting mistakes.

Always remember that the investing world is a human world, and the skills and abilities that have served us so well in understanding and developing our material surroundings don't necessarily translate very well. Our answers can't all be found on a spreadsheet; they need inner view as well as outer.

In addition to self-awareness, strategy and discipline can neutralize the behavioral minefields raised in investment. In an unknowable world, we believe the best way is taking the long view—finding and holding high-quality companies that generate dividend income now and continually grow their dividends over time. In our opinion, our strategic and disciplined approach is "therapy" for the behavioral finance mistakes caused by impulsive emotional investing.

Lowell G. Miller

About the author

Lowell G. Miller, CIO, founded Miller/Howard in 1984. He began his studies of the securities markets as an undergraduate and has continuously pursued the notion of disciplined investment strategies since 1976. He is author of three acclaimed books on investing, including The Single Best Investment: Creating Wealth with Dividend Growth (Print Project, 2nd Edition, 2006). He has also written on financial topics for The New York Times Magazine, and has been a featured guest on Louis Rukeyser's Wall $treet Week and Bloomberg TV.

Lowell is frequently quoted in financial media such as the Wall Street Journal, Dow Jones Newswires, Bloomberg, Fortune, and Barron's. He holds a BA in Philosophy from Sarah Lawrence College and a Juris Doctor degree from New York University School of Law.

About Miller/Howard Investments

Miller/Howard Investments Inc. is an independent, SEC registered investment firm with over two decades' experience managing equity portfolios for institutions and individuals in disciplined, dividend-focused investment strategies. We invest in companies across the broad market that our investment team identifies as financially strong with the ability to pay and consistently raise dividends. Our portfolio strategies include: income-equity broad market stocks, master limited partnerships (MLPs), utilities, infrastructure, and "Drill Bit to Burner Tip®" components of the North American energy value chain.

Financial Freedom and Retirement

Financial freedom, as I would define it, can be achieved in two ways. The first, winning an eye-watering amount of cash at high-stakes poker or on the lottery, both incredibly unlikely as I have little interest in either. The second, and much more realistic route to financial freedom, is my retirement – the point at which I have saved enough money to maintain my lifestyle for the remainder of my days without the need to continue working.

Don't get me wrong, I enjoy my work and I'm very ambitious when it comes to my career and making a positive difference for my employer, our client's and with my colleagues. However, I also value my own time and recognise the need to be disciplined in order to maintain a quality work/life balance. I definitely sit in the 'work to live' camp but do get tremendous satisfaction from a successful work life. I have a busy personal life and always enjoy trying new things. In recent years I have taken up art, playing the piano, cycling and even playing the bagpipes – a somewhat eclectic mix of hobbies and not all met with universal appreciation by my family!

Working with a company who specialise in retirement planning has taught me that it is not just the financial aspects of retirement that we need to plan for – we also need to be retirement-ready mentally. The change from full-time work to not working at all is a drastic one and I've heard many tales of clients who simply were not ready to retire and it takes them months and sometimes years to adjust. Having seen these problems and hearing of other client tales where they have adapted to retirement extremely well, I feel comfortable I have the outlook, hobbies and social infrastructure to be retirement-ready when the time comes.

While I know it's a bit of a cliché, I am a firm believer we only get one chance on this planet and the barrier to seeing and doing more is always going to be time. While working hard and playing hard appears to be the best philosophy for me right now, with additional time I know I could do more of the things I would like to be doing and are of greater importance to me. To access and enjoy more time for myself, I need to first be comfortable I have achieved financial freedom.

Many of us are influenced by the direction our parents' lives have taken and my parents' retirement has undoubtedly shaped the aspirations I have for my own retirement. My Mum and Dad are both now in their 70s, having retired in their mid to late 50s, and are thoroughly enjoying themselves. They are blessed with good health and their retirement is quite simply one big exciting holiday. They have, and continue to travel the world, enjoy a wide variety of hobbies, are frequently trying new things and have a wide social circle to engage with. They have shown me what a good retirement looks like; and long may it continue. The question I now ask myself is how can I achieve a similar retirement outcome for my wife and I?

I am also a realist; retiring early is a major challenge. I recognise life expectancy is increasing, I have a certain standard of living I want to achieve and I understand there are risks and factors which could throw my retirement plans to the winds. My goal therefore is to have enough financial resources to fund my retirement goals and an additional safety net in case circumstances or plans happen to change along the way.

Before I get on to the how, a little more background about me.

I am in my late 40s (I've avoided saying nearly 50!), married and have one child who in theory is non-dependant but that's another of my great plans which has been well and truly thrown to the winds. I have been working in Financial Services since graduating from University and employed by a number of well-known financial organisations. Along the way I have accrued different pension arrangements, including a small final salary pension and a number of different defined contribution pensions. At the simplest level, my final salary pension will pay me a guaranteed pension at 60, based on my years of service and salary at the date of leaving. My defined contribution pensions on the other hand are where I take on all the risks and my pension fund and future income is based on how much money has been paid in and how the pension investments perform. I also had a couple of relatively short employments where I ended up receiving a refund of contributions and no pension benefits because I had been employed for less than two years. Overall, I have a mixed bag of pension benefits, as I'm sure most people do, and I had never really taken my own 'retirement planning' seriously until the day I started working at specialist retirement planning advisers, Intelligent Pensions.

While I may not have been focused on my retirement planning prior to joining the company, like any good Scotsman, I have always watched the pennies and been reasonably financially savvy. Like many younger people, buying a house had been my major financial priority and once settled in a family home, my focus turned to paying off the mortgage. Besides my time at University, I have been fortunate not to need to take on any debt – no personal loans or credit cards eating away at my net pay, so my mortgage was the only debt I needed to focus on. Having an interest only mortgage means I save to ISAs (was previously PEPs) to act as the repayment vehicle. I also found I was saving money in the Bank which meant I could look at off-set mortgages and I decided it was the perfect solution to meet my objectives. Tax benefits and reduced interest payments by offsetting my mortgage debt against my bank balances, while still retaining the flexibility to access funds should I ever need them.

So, to be clear, I haven't paid my mortgage off and don't have to for another 10 years but thanks to a few bonuses and some diligent saving I now pay little or no interest to the bank every month and for all intents and purposes, and certainly in my own mind, my mortgage is dealt with. Plus, I still have the ISAs which can now be used for my retirement planning rather than having to pay off the mortgage.

When I joined Intelligent Pensions, I felt I had a good knowledge about pensions generally but very little knowledge or understanding about how adequate my own pension savings were or what they were on track to achieve.

As Marketing Director, I naturally threw myself into the service proposition and client experience by attending client meetings and reading client file reviews and reports. This exposed me to a wide variety of client retirement plans and their different attitudes and expectations of retirement. I continue to review and see many examples of clients who have made mistakes and are unlikely to achieve the optimal retirement outcome. Some simply haven't saved enough and risk running out of money while others must compromise their retirement objectives either by spending less or working longer. On the other side of the coin there are those who have saved far more than they are ever going to spend and could perhaps have retired earlier or can afford to live more lavishly.

I very quickly realised that I didn't want to fall on either side of the fence of saving too little or too much and to give myself the best chance of achieving my financial freedom objectives through retirement, I needed a plan, and a good one.

Firstly, I had to face the million-dollar retirement planning questions:

- What age do I want to retire?
- How much annual income will I need in retirement?
- How long will I be in retirement for?
- What other income sources do I have available?
- How much money overall will I need to save?
- Do I want to pass down any of my wealth to family members?
- How much can I currently afford to save?
- Am I on track to achieve my retirement objectives?

My initial answers to the majority of these questions were "no idea" and I am sure I'm not the only one who would have to respond in kind.

So many questions, all a moving feast and some impossible to answer. To be honest, I probably wouldn't even have contemplated any of these questions if I hadn't joined a specialist retirement advice business, let alone have any idea about how to answer them.

I should confess at this point, I am not a qualified financial adviser and these are my thoughts and plans which may not be entirely sensible and probably not in the best interests of others. But they work for me and are giving me a focus towards my goal of financial freedom. In addition, while I refer to 'I' and 'my' a lot, all my financial arrangements and retirement plans are on a joint basis with my wife.

The biggest dilemma and unknown for those retiring is when they are going to die. Most people will typically underestimate their life expectancy and while there are tools which can help to give you an average life expectancy what if you are the lucky or unlucky one, depending on how you look at it, who dies well before or lives way beyond the average? The average is therefore always likely to be wrong but the issue is by how much?

For what it's worth I tried one of the online life expectancy calculators, avoiding the aptly named 'deathclock' and after entering some basic details, it calculated my life expectancy as age 90. Although this is interesting to know, it is not something to plan for.

If we could spend all our savings before a known death date, life would be ever so simple. I know there are options in this regard but not options I'm ready to contemplate just yet. So how do you solve the problem of longevity? In truth, the only way to do so is to insure yourself against living too long which can be achieved by buying an annuity – a guaranteed income for life. But who wants to buy an annuity? Rates are low and following George Osborne's infamous speech where he stated 'nobody will ever have to buy an annuity' annuities have been significantly tarnished in the minds of consumers. That said, I do have a respect for longevity and recognise I may need some security later in life. Possibly when I'm in my 70's an annuity might be a sensible option to consider.

The second question I struggled with was one I thought would be relatively simple. How much money would we need in retirement? To be honest, I struggled to work out what we spend currently never mind what we might be spending in 20, 30 or 40 year's time. With the help of an online budget planner, I did get to a sensible figure for our current essential and desirable expenditure but found that this was only of limited use when forecasting our future expenditure. How would our spending patterns change in retirement? How much money would I save if I was not working? And how much more would we want to spend to enjoy retirement on things like holidays and hobbies?

There are many 'rules of thumb' when it comes to what replacement income you need in retirement and naturally this is influenced greatly by the amount you earn and your spending patterns. In the end, I have set myself a target of 67% replacement income (two thirds of my current net take-home pay) in retirement which I am comfortable would be enough to achieve our desired standard of living.

In addition to this level of regular income, I want to have access to some additional lump sums every 5 years from 60 through to 70 to fund items such as car purchase, home improvements, special holidays and any other unforeseen items of expenditure.

Building My Retirement Cashflow Model

The next stage of my planning was to do some cashflow modelling. This is what clients I have met with have found most engaging and helped them to understand and visualise their retirement in a way that words can simply never achieve. Pensions and retirement planning can be complex and the adage 'a picture paints a thousand words' has never been truer when it comes to cashflow modelling and retirement planning.

At its most basic level, building a cashflow model involves mapping current and future income sources against long-term income requirements, taking account of ongoing inflation.

I checked with the Government website (www.gov.uk/check-state-pension) to find my state pension age and entitlements and logged into my pension and investment online accounts to get up to date valuations. All my pensions, with the exception of the very small final salary defined benefit pension, are now consolidated in a self-invested personal pension (SIPP) which I set up to benefit from increased investment choice, lower overall charges and the simplicity of having everything under one roof. The only other investments I have are my ISAs and some bank shares from a previous long-term incentive plan.

To do effective cashflow modelling I needed to set a target retirement age. To a point, I'm happy to be quite flexible about this but I have a very clear objective to achieve financial freedom by the age of 60. If I can achieve it sooner, that's all well and good but 60 is the hard backstop. That doesn't necessarily mean I will retire at 60 but I want to have the option to.

The base line of my retirement plan is shown in cashflow model 1 and is based on me retiring at the backstop age 60. The model is based on the financial resources and income requirements for both my wife and I.

CASHFLOW MODEL 1

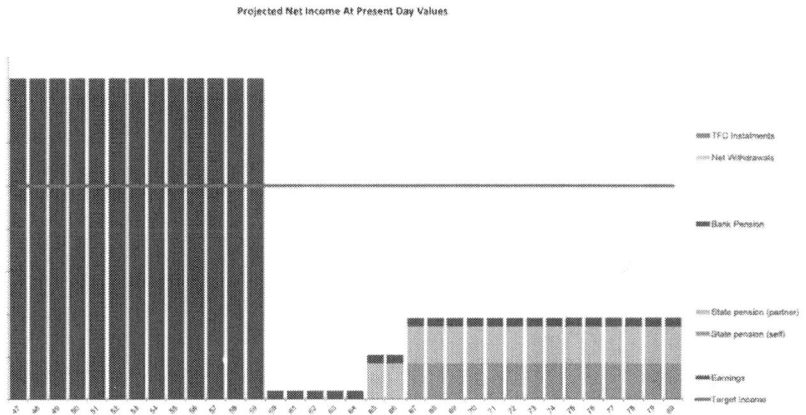

Projected Net Income At Present Day Values

As you can see, my earnings fall away at 60 and my small DB pension scheme comes into payment. My wife is older than me so her state pension comes in when I'm 65 and then my state pension commences at age 67. My target 67% income is shown by the target income line. To achieve financial freedom, I therefore need my SIPP, and other investments, to be able to fill in the white areas between my target income and the income I will be receiving, plus be capable of providing the additional lump sums I want at 60, 65 and 70.

My projected SIPP value is now entered to see if it can meet my objectives – cashflow model 2.

CASHFLOW MODEL 2

Projected Net Income At Present Day Values

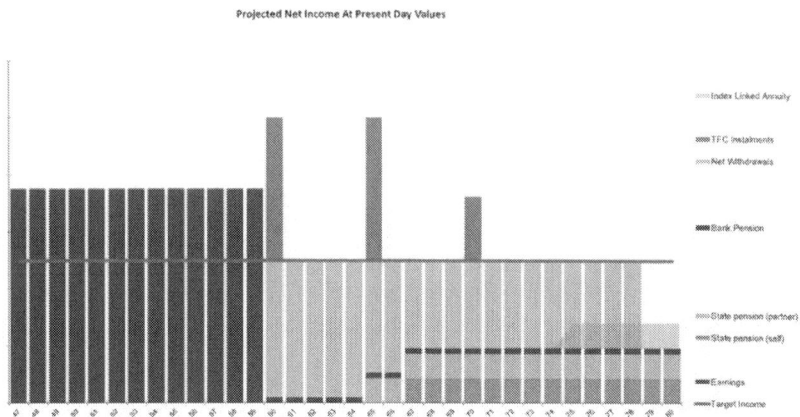

The pink spikes show tax-free cash (TFC) being taken and the Manchester City blue (yes, I am a fan) shows the net income withdrawals from my SIPP. Under this scenario, I would be short of my desired additional cash at age 70, my pension would run out at age 78 and I would be more than 40% short of my income target – not a terribly attractive option.

The yellow shading from age 75 provides an indication what index-linked annuity the remainder of my pension funds could purchase and, in this case, it isn't very much at all! The estimated annuity rate at age 75 is just 5.62% so perhaps it isn't hard to see why annuities are so unpopular just now. Cashflow model 2 doesn't take account of my ongoing pension contributions through to retirement, so these are now added into the analysis to give the result in cashflow model 3 on the next page.

CASHFLOW MODEL 3

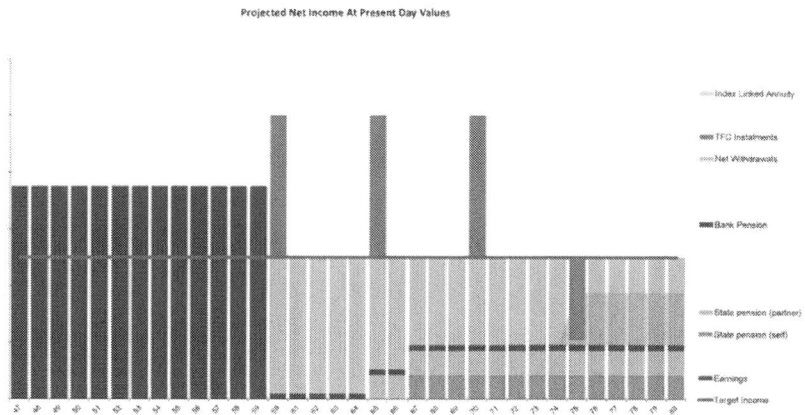

Projected Net Income At Present Day Values

The picture is starting to look much better but caution is needed as the modeller is only forecasting to age 80. Looking at the future analysis, my pension would be exhausted at age 86. Buying an index-linked annuity at age 75 would also result in almost a 40% income shortfall from 75 onwards. The modeller estimates I would need an additional £282,000 in my fund at age 75 to buy the required level of index-linked annuity. To close this shortfall, I would need to contribute an additional £17,500 per annum into my pension for the next 13 years. I did say I could save more money but nothing to that extent so what other options do I have?

The main additional resource I want to use for my retirement is my investments. As my ISAs and shares are no longer needed to pay down the mortgage, they can now be used to support my retirement objectives.

My retirement model is assuming a net investment growth rate of 2.8% p.a. for my pension (more about that later) so I apply the same growth rate to provide a sustainable level of income that can be taken from my predicted ISA and investments value. This is considered in cashflow model 4 below.

CASHFLOW MODEL 4

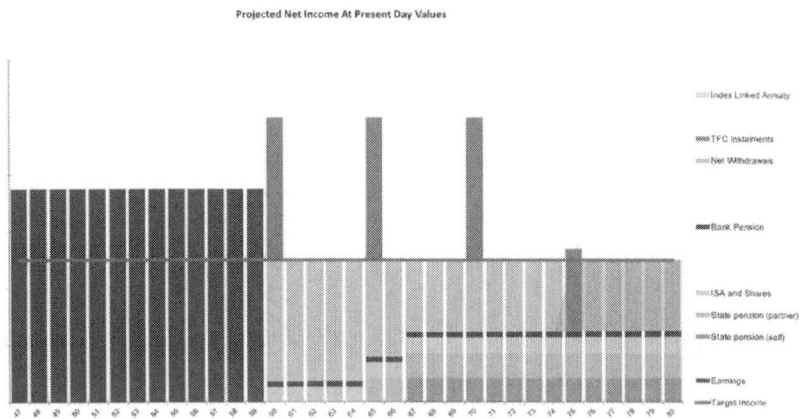

Projected Net Income At Present Day Values

As can now be seen, I actually have a small amount of excess tax-free cash at age 75 which can either be spent or reinvested for additional retirement income. The yellow shaded area, which indicates potential income to come from an index-linked annuity, is now enough to meet my income target. Whether I choose to access my pension funds through drawdown or opt to buy an annuity, my retirement plans look to be achievable. Provided all the cashflow modelling assumptions hold true, of course.

One of the biggest assumptions in any cashflow model is investment performance. Along with longevity and inflation, investment performance is the hardest part to predict. My cashflow model is based on a net investment growth rate after inflation and charges of 2.8% p.a. This reflects my above average attitude towards investment risk which I am comfortable taking given the relatively long investment horizon and equates to 87% of my pension fund being exposed to equity investments. This exposure is achieved by investing in approximately 20 funds to provide the required asset allocation and desired geographical split.

To test my cashflow model against a market crash, I introduce a 30% fall in stock markets with no immediate recovery, similar to that seen in the financial crisis of 2008. The result of such an event is shown in cashflow model 5.

CASHFLOW MODEL 5

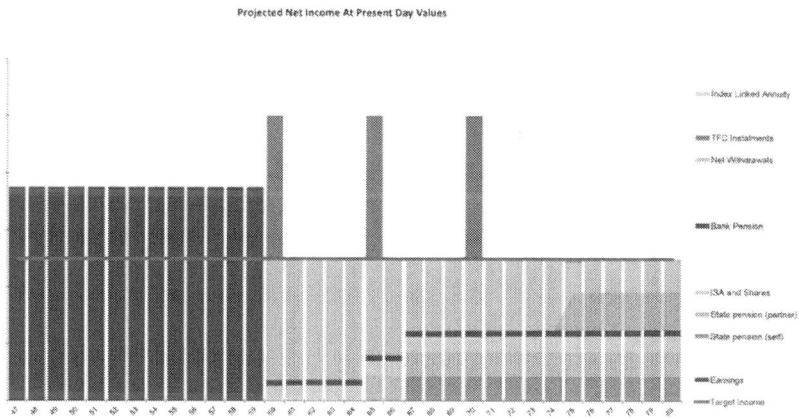

Projected Net Income At Present Day Values

In cashflow model 5 we can now see that the index-linked annuity (yellow shading) route would result in a 25% shortfall in my retirement income and if I stayed in income drawdown, the fund is forecast to be exhausted by age 84.

This demonstrates the very real investment risk faced by people with defined contribution pensions and income drawdown plans. Adverse market movements can and will play a significant part in achieving my retirement objectives and while completely outside of my control, they are something I must pay ongoing attention to.

Finally, for my own interests, I wanted to see how my cashflow model would look if I retired earlier, at age 58. So, going back to cashflow model 4, I readjust the figures to retire at age 58 and the outcome is shown in cashflow model 6.

CASHFLOW MODEL 6

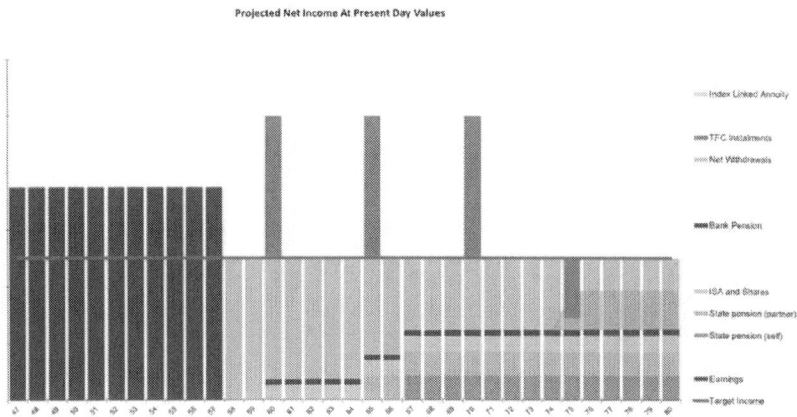

Projected Net Income At Present Day Values

Retiring at age 58 looks like a challenge. My cashflow model is now predicting a shortfall of £253,000 at age 75 to buy the required index-linked annuity.

To address the shortfall, the modeller has indicated that annual contributions of £20,000 p.a. would be required for the next 11 years. The additional contributions are beyond what I could save just now and would potentially give rise to some annual allowance (AA) and future lifetime allowance (LTA) issues.

By way of a brief and simplistic explanation, the lifetime allowance is the maximum you can have in your pension. Any pension funds above this limit may attract a lifetime allowance charge of up to 55%. The lifetime allowance for the 2019/2020 tax year is £1,055,000 and is set to rise by CPI (consumer price index) measure each year. The annual allowance is designed to limit how much tax-relief the Treasury (HMT) pays on pension contributions and effectively limits how much people pay in. For most people the allowance is £40,000 p.a. but for higher earners it is restricted even further.

One asset that hasn't been evaluated in any of the cashflow analysis is my wife's pension. While she does qualify for a full state pension, her own personal pension is negligible, hence not included in the cashflow analysis, and she isn't currently in paid employment. One further option therefore is that I contribute £3,600 p.a. to her personal pension in the knowledge it can be drawn down, particularly in the early years, to take advantage of her tax-free personal allowance. £3,600 is the maximum amount that can be paid into a pension and benefit from tax relief where the pension holder does not have any earnings. The actual cost of this £3,600 contribution is only £2,880 and the pension provider will reclaim the £720 tax relief from the Treasury.

The Backstop

The one thing that could have a significant adverse impact on my plans is my health, both in the short term if it prevents me from working and therefore earning and in the longer term through the possible need for long-term care. While insurance can be an effective solution to mitigate the first issue, the second is far more difficult and from my experience, people are far less willing to make provision for long-term care.

While it might not be the perfect answer, I do still have my house which could be used to generate income or capital in retirement. Also, should I be fortunate enough to have a long life expectancy, that would increase the likelihood of receiving an inheritance or two. As such, I feel these last resort options are sufficient to act as the backstop should my health deteriorate and additional income or capital is needed to be found.

In the event of something more severe, namely my premature death, my wife would inherit all my investments, including my SIPP. She wouldn't be entitled to as much income from my Bank pension but existing life insurance would more than compensate for the loss. In the event of my wife's premature death, I too would benefit from life insurance and believe a reduced income requirement would offset the loss of her state pension.

The Alternatives

There are a host of alternative strategies and routes I could consider to achieve financial freedom and my retirement objectives but using my pension and other tax-efficient savings is the route I feel comfortable with and is most easily accessible to me.

Many people reading this will probably be screaming 'buy some rental property' but in all honesty, the thought of owning more property sends a chill down my spine. Should anything break or go wrong in our house, I panic and have little idea about what to do to fix it. Fortunately, my Dad is extremely handy and still able to come to the rescue but with all his holidays and other pastimes, getting him booked in is like getting an appointment with your Doctor! So, the thought of owning another property holds zero attraction for me, not to mention the increased stamp duty costs and less attractive tax regime owning a second property now endures.

I also put my trust and faith in others to make my investments. Despite holding investment qualifications and previously running an investment club, my experience has taught me I simply don't know enough. Mistakes are just too easy to make and too hard to recover from, especially the older you get. My more recent direct equity purchases have all suffered significant losses and I now recognise I don't have the time, skill or desire to try and pick stocks, I'm much better off leaving that to the experts who do have the time and experience.

Summary

Overall, I am confident that I am on track to achieve financial freedom through my retirement plans. But it is only having gone through a cashflow modelling exercise that has given me this confidence. Clearly my circumstances and external markets will continue to change and I recognise that revisiting my plan on a regular basis is essential to ensure it remains fit for purpose.

The vast majority of people in the UK, like me, will look to achieve financial freedom in retirement. With the absence of defined benefit pensions, low average pension savings and the pushing back of the state pension age, the number of people who will achieve it, and at a level of desired income, is likely to be the small minority. Initiatives such as Auto Enrolment, which requires all employers to provide and fund a pension for their employees, are making a positive contribution to pension savings but are nowhere near the funding levels required to achieve reasonable replacement income in retirement.

One of the biggest problems with pensions is engagement. People find the language alien and complex and in general, pensions are a problem for the future. Very few people have any idea what their pension savings represent or if they are on track to achieve their objectives and these two simple pieces of knowledge are key drivers of engagement and action to help people effectively target financial freedom through retirement. The Government has proposed a mid-life MOT which is an excellent idea to help people engage with their pensions at a time when they still have some ability to act.

For me, the biggest disconnect is between pension savings and the need for professional advice. Advice should not be confused with guidance, the latter telling you lots of things you could do whereas advice is telling you what you should do. In the same way you, or at least I, wouldn't try to re-wire my house, fix my boiler or self-diagnose the pain in my lower back, people shouldn't be left on their own to understand how their pensions work and whether they are on track to achieve their goals.

The cashflow modelling I have described is relatively simple but it would still be very easy to make a mistake or mis-understand the inputs and/or outputs. What my experience has shown me is that most of us need an expert to help us navigate the cashflow modelling – to challenge our assumptions and objectives and direct us towards better retirement outcomes and a better chance of achieving financial freedom.

Andrew Pennie

About the author

Besides the fact I'm quite tall, bald and have what I consider to be a healthy outlook on life, I suspect I've probably told you as much about me as you would ever wish to know.

As a very brief summary, I am in my late 40's and I'm married with one child in their 20's. I have been working in Financial Services since graduating from University. I am the marketing director at leading retirement income specialists, Intelligent Pensions. I have worked in financial services since graduating from University for over 25 years and for a number of household brands, including Santander, Ernst & Young, Lloyds and HSBC.

I graduated from Hull University with a BSc Honours Degree in Accountancy and hold a number of financial services qualifications.

The Secrets Of A Successful Retirement

If the secret to a happy retirement is simply how much money a retiree has there would be a lot of happy, wealthy people and a larger number of unhappy, less wealthy people all of retirement age. But this isn't the case. There is much research and evidence to show there isn't a strong correlation between wealth and happiness. In fact, the evidence is that one's financial position contributes to happiness to a point but beyond a certain level of income, about $75,000 pa, the relationship breaks down[1].

It is also the case that in the Western world particularly we have developed an unhealthy relationship with money: we can worry about it, be intimidated by it and obsess about it. But the truth is money has no inherent value; it's just a medium to facilitate the exchange of goods and services. To prove it try being shipwrecked with just a wallet full of pounds or dollars. It won't get you very far, a fishing rod and a water purification system would be much more valuable. A sailing boat would be better still.

There are also many examples of lottery winners who have hit the jackpot only to wish they could revert to their pre-lottery lifestyle. They found the sudden increase in wealth didn't bring about lasting happiness, but it did lead to relationship strains and other non-financial complexities. Indeed, a 1970s piece of research[2] that compared the happiness of Illinois State lottery winners with those who suffered from a life changing accident found that, on a relative basis there wasn't much difference in happiness between the two groups. The reason for the similarity is what psychologists refer to as the

---

[1] Source: 'High income improves evaluation of life but not emotional well-being'; Kahnemann & Deaton 2010.

[2] Source: Lottery winners and accident victims: Is happiness relative? Brickman, P., Coates, D., & Janoff-Bulman, R. (1978)

'hedonic treadmill' or 'hedonic adaptation'. The lottery winners would upgrade their lifestyles to suit their new wealth, but it didn't have an equal effect on their happiness, it simply became the new normal. On the other hand, those who suffered a catastrophic injury placed a greater value on life's simple pleasures having revalued what was and was not important to them.

With life expectancy increasing with advances in medicine and a better understanding of what makes a healthy lifestyle the duration of retirement is substantially more than when the concept of retirement was first introduced. According to current longevity statistics[3] someone who is forty now has a 50:50 chance of living to age ninety-five and today's fifty-year-olds have a 50:50 chance of living to ninety. With retirement now more likely to be a multi-decade phase rather than a multi-year phase, for it to be lived successfully the retiree needs to navigate physical, mental and emotional changes.

We go through a difficult transition from childhood to adulthood called adolescence. It's a time of trying to understand who we are and our place in a complicated world while at the same time changing physically, emotionally and mentally.

We ask ourselves, who am I? Where am I going? What is important? What am I going to do?

Perhaps the transition from working life to retirement is no different? For the first time in 40 years or so we are faced with wholesale change. We change physically as our bodies grow older and life is full of unknowns; different expectations of others and by others, different identity and status and our long-held relationships face new challenges. Again, we may be asking questions of ourselves: who am I? Where am I going? What is important? What am I going to do?

---

[3] 'The 100 Year Life'; Gratton & Scott

So, if money has no inherent value and having lots of it doesn't guarantee happiness, what then determines whether retirement can be deemed 'successful' or not?

In nearly twenty years in financial services, half of that time as a financial planner, I have had many conversations with clients about retirement and have conducted my own research on the subject. In my experience there are five factors that have a direct influence on whether an individual can be said to have retired successfully:

1. they are in a loving relationship,
2. they are healthy and active,
3. they are part of a social network or community,
4. they have a sense of purpose and,
5. they have the peace of mind that comes with financial security.

No single factor alone can determine a successful retirement but struggling in one area can have a negative consequence overall.

The rest of this chapter looks at each of these areas in turn and draws upon existing research and my own experience as a financial planner specialising in helping people transition into retirement.

1. Loving Relationships

There is a great deal of evidence to show that the quality of a marital or long-term relationship is a major influence on the quality of one's retirement. During working-life, with much of the week being spent out of the house, couples have space and time away from each other but in retirement the home can feel like a more confined place with two people spending more time in each other's company.

This proximity can lead to small irritations that were previously not observed or not relevant but, overtime can cause conflict. According to the Office for National Statistics, in the UK the rate of divorce decreased in 2018 compared to 2017 but rates remained level for couples aged 60 and over. Reasons often cited being that couples wait for children to be financially independent and out of full time education before separating but also, linked to increased longevity, the prospect of a further twenty to thirty years of marriage feels too much to manage and the need for a fresh start becomes too appealing to ignore.

Where, historically, it has been the husband who has been the bread winner and the wife the homemaker, having the husband coming into the wife's domain and interfering with her routine can be too much to bear. It's not hard to imagine that comments along the lines of *"What are you doing?"*, *"why are you doing it that way? I'd do it this way"* would soon become antagonising.

Or as a divorced client once commented to me:

"it's better to be happily divorced than unhappily married."

There is even statistical evidence to bear this out: according to a 2017 research paper[4] on happiness, a married retiree with a poor relationship has a lower life satisfaction compared to those who are not married. There needs to be an 43% improvement in leisure quality and satisfaction to be as happy as an unmarried retiree and double that for a high-quality spousal relationship.

Those who I have spoken to that do enjoy a happy marriage throughout retirement put the success down to a mutual respect of each other's independence and the need to balance doing things together and apart.

---

[4] Spending, Relationship Quality, and Life Satisfaction in Retirement, Finke, Ho & Huston (2017).

2. Being Active & Healthy

There can be no surprise that the body atrophies with time, with the greatest effects being felt beyond the age of 60. And, even though medical advances are enabling the global population as a whole to live longer, physical and mental decline in retirement will have a significant bearing on the quality of that phase of life.

Being active and healthy is a virtuous circle; the more active and healthier you become the more active and healthier you can be and so on.

According to the National Health Service (NHS) in the UK, there is a strong link between inactivity and heart related diseases, cancers, strokes, diabetes as well as mental illnesses. The benefits of an active lifestyle are more than just physical; simply being outdoors is known to enhance mental wellbeing too. Or to quote the Roman poet Juvenal, "Mens sana in corpore sano" which translates to the more well-known phrase:

"A healthy mind in a healthy body".

The NHS recommends two and a half hours of moderate activity each week, which can be as simple as gardening, walking or yoga rather than more exerting activities such as swimming, running or cycling.

Physical activity should be more than increasing heart health, it is also important to maintain muscle strength in later life too. The NHS states heart health, bone strength, lower blood sugar levels and lower blood pressure as benefits of maintaining muscle mass. As with aerobic activity this doesn't require tough gym sessions, lighter but regular activity that gets the muscles working can be enough to maintain strength as you age.

Nutrition also plays an important role in vitality in retirement. As the human body's ability to process fat declines with age the quality of food that is consumed is of greater importance if heart related illnesses are to be minimised. A healthy diet is not hard to maintain if a few simple practices are followed each day which balances a mix of fruit, vegetables, fish, pulses and meats but still allows for treats to be enjoyed in moderation[5]. The good news is that it doesn't have to be fresh food prepared daily, there is evidence that tinned food is as nutritious as fresh alternatives[6].

Alcohol consumption needs to be managed in retirement too if related illnesses are to be avoided. The freedom of not having to go to work in the morning can also mean that more 'excuses' to have 'another' drink can creep in, especially if alcohol helps fill a void in the day. Guidance from the UK Government is to limit weekly consumption to 14 units a week or the equivalent of six 568 ml pints of beer, six 175 ml glasses of wine or twelve 25ml glasses of spirits.

3. Being Part of a Community

Homo Sapiens are social animals that require a social network to belong to. Our early ancestors depended on each other to forage, hunt and share childcare duties. It also enabled the development of storytelling, gossip and teaching that helped create larger communities and religions. Following the agricultural revolution communities also got together to help manage farming demands throughout the year, particularly at harvest time which was a time of collective labour but also of celebration.

During working life our needs for social stimuli can be met in the workplace. Without a replacement network in place these needs can be harder to meet resulting in feelings of boredom, loneliness and, ultimately for some, can be a cause of depression. As a retired judge explained to me, the biggest mistake can be to go back to work to visit old colleagues; you will probably find that old friends, whilst pleased to see you, are too busy to stop to talk with life having moved on.

---

[5] https://www.ageuk.org.uk/information-advice/health-wellbeing/healthy-eating/healthy-eating-guide/
[6] www.canned.co.uk.

The change in working patterns has allowed workers to retire gradually by reducing working hours and commitments over several years to help the transition for both the employee and employer. There is also the opportunity to take on Non-executive director and chairperson roles so that the freedom of retirement can be counterbalanced with the need to stay mentally stimulated and, perhaps, have another source of income until State sponsored pensions commence.

Those who have successfully retired enjoy an active social life that centres around an interest or hobby. That might be an activity that has always been a source of enjoyment but work and family life prevented it from being pursued with any regularity or a new one that has been picked up since retiring and provides the opportunity for social connections.

I have experienced first-hand the joy that can be felt when communities get together on a regular basis. The small English village in which I live has several occasions throughout the year when residents of all ages, from families with new-born babies to octogenarian widows and widowers get together. The topics of conversation will be different from that of our early hunter-gatherer ancestors, but the purpose remains the same: to share stories, gossip and be entertained.

4. Having a Sense of Purpose

Retirement can either be viewed as retiring 'from' something or retiring 'to' something and depending upon the lens it is viewed from can lead to a different retirement experience. If it is a case of retiring 'from' something there may be a difficult void to fill if there is nothing to replace work. I heard of a doctor who was forced to retire when his business partner decided to but, because he wasn't ready to retire and had nothing to fill the gap, he went from having a healthy interest in wine and a love of golf to having no interest in golf and an unhealthy interest in wine.

Those who have successfully retired have done so because they have an alternative source of fulfilment, a sense of purpose and a reason to get up in the morning.

In their book, The 100 Year Life, the authors Lynda Gratton & Andrew Scott explain that with increased longevity comes a longer period of retirement (assuming a lack of financial resources don't require a like-for-like increase in working life) which is likely to necessitate a *re-creation* of the retiree because a life of *recreation* may soon become unfulfilling. As the doctor referenced above found, the novelty of being able to play golf every day will soon wear-off and boredom soon set in[7]. Or to put it another way, *"when you have a jar full of cookies, where's the fun in cookies?"*[8]

Authors talk about the difficult second book and musicians, the difficult second album. Retirees should also think about the difficult second year. The first year is novel; nobody is telling you where to be at what time, and you have the freedom and opportunity to do what you want to do. However, once that novelty has worn off year two can be harder to manage: there is time to fill, particularly during the cold, wet and dark winter months. One also tends to forget the negative parts of work but recall fondly the enjoyable aspects; the friends, having a purpose and job satisfaction.

This period of re-creation is about more than just having activities to fill the time, it's about creating a new identity for oneself. As suggested at the start of this chapter, retirement is, perhaps, also a second adolescence when retirees need to re-discover who they are. I've had conversations with retirees who have admitted to finding the loss of status after a successful career hard to manage. The retired judge referenced earlier is a man of very little ego but acknowledged that going from a position of status and authority to "just" a retired person was hard to get used to.

---

[7] For a list of 101 things to do in retirement to avoid getting bored visit: https://neliganfinancial.co.uk/101things-boredom/
[8] To quote actor Martin Clunes in the hit 1990s sitcom, Men Behaving Badly, albeit in a different context

Sandler Training® founder David Sandler came up with the Identity/Role (I/R) theory to help salespeople around the world understand that their success or failure as a salesperson doesn't affect who they are as a person. This can apply equally to retirees. Everyone has a sense of identity that, in theory, should be positive, the problem occurs when an individual's sense of self is affected by success or failure in their role. A bad day in the office doesn't make you a worse father/mother/wife/husband/friend/person but someone with low identity may feel that way.

At retirement the loss of role can lead to a lowering in identity if you defined yourself by what you did rather than who you were. A recent study of US professionals and their views on retirement by Harvard Professor Teresa Amabile found that that those who prepared for retirement in a psychological and relationship sense as well as a financial sense found the transition into retirement a smoother one and less likely to find the early honeymoon period wearing off.

5. Financial Security

I started this chapter by stating that money is a means to an end and that having a lot of it doesn't guarantee happiness. However, the peace of mind that comes with knowing you have *enough* money to live, come what may, can be an important factor in determining whether a retirement is successful or not.

Having worked hard for 40 odd years and having become accustomed to a particular lifestyle it will be hard to adjust to anything less than ideal when faced with more time freedom. I don't know many people who seek a lifestyle upgrade in retirement, except, perhaps, for extra spending on travel and leisure, but most people I speak to don't want a lifestyle downgrade.

I'm regularly asked what size pension is needed to fund someone's retirement. It is a simple question in theory but not a simple one to answer because it really does depend upon so many factors. The greatest variable being the cost of one's ideal retirement lifestyle; if you live the lifestyle of a highly paid sportsman or actor the pot needed to fund it when the career finishes will be vastly greater than the pot needed for someone who neither wants or needs much in their life.

We are in a transition phase for retirees; many current retirees are enjoying the guaranteed security of a company pension payable for life with annual inflationary linked increases but with most company schemes now closed more and more retirees are those that have to self-fund their retirement. The self-funded retiree must make sure they are taking appropriate action soon enough to grow their wealth to a level that can sustain a thirty-year plus retirement. It also requires a level of wealth that allows for multi-decade increases in the cost of living which, if not planned for carefully, substantially diminishes the purchasing power of their wealth.

When considering the questions of "how much is enough?" and "where's the money going to come from?" the prepared individual will start their retirement planning early enough so that they have time for the majesty of compound interest to grow their wealth. Having a big enough pot enables them to fund the early, typically more active, years of retirement with enough left for the later years when the cost of travel and leisure may reduce but the real-terms cost of living has increased and the spectre of later life care becomes a factor.

The self-funded retiree must also contend with the vagaries of the investment markets and decide how much investment risk they are willing and can afford to take with their hard-earned nest-eggs. On the one hand, too much investment risk coupled with higher lifestyle costs risks irreparable depletion during stock market crashes. On the other hand, a too cautious approach risks the pension and investment pots not keeping up with neither regular withdrawals nor the long-term negative effects of inflation.

A worthwhile exercise when planning and funding retirement is to review one's expenditure to work out what regular costs are essential, valued and not valued. Those clients who have gone through the financial process and audited their spending[9] have found it a worthwhile and illuminating exercise. By re-directing the non-essential and non-valued expenses to either funding retirement or removing them completely, the potential for financial security in retirement can increase greatly.

Financial security is also not a single person issue, couples need to know that the survivor will be financially secure on the death of the first person and also, for many, that children can also be given a start to adult life by assisting them with deposits for their first house or help with debts accrued as students.

Enjoying a successful retirement can be like juggling, failing to focus on one of the five factors outlined in this chapter can lead to you dropping the ball which may lead to more of them falling. Failure to tend to your relationship resulting in a breakdown could lead to health-related issues and perhaps a detachment from social groups or meaningful activities. Or, having a lack of purpose and a tendency to drift through days could lead to melancholy which could lead to health issues and ultimately relationship strains. As US financial planner and speaker Mitch Anthony says: *"A life of ease is two steps from a life of disease".*

We don't know what curve balls life may throw at us; we all probably know of someone who had their retirement cut short by death too soon after stopping work. Somethings we can't plan for but the more we do to prepare ourselves financially, physically, psychologically and emotionally for the next phases of our lives the greater the chance we have of enjoying a long and successful retirement.

Andrew Neligan

---

[9] If you would like to review your expenditure visit:
https://neliganfinancial.co.uk/expenditure-questionnaire-protected/

About the author

Andrew Neligan is a Chartered Financial Planner and Certified Financial Planner™ who runs his own financial planning business, Neligan Financial, which helps his clients prepare and transition into retirement. He lives in Devon, south west England with his wife Carol and two children, Edward and Holly.

The Benefits of Peer-to-Peer Lending

What does financial freedom look like to you?

Getting clarity on what the term "financial freedom" means to you is the first step to figuring out where you want to go and how much you would like to get you there.

Once you have figured out the end goal, the rest can be fun and is not as hard as you might think.

What do the following words mean to you?

- o Abundance
- o Wealth
- o Freedom

Take a few minutes to note down a few ideas about each word and see what comes up for you. You could write words or doodle, whichever feels more natural to you. The object here is to engage your brain, get clarity on what you want to achieve and to focus on your big WHY. This big why is your purpose for wanting financial freedom.

Your big WHY is important. It is what will get you out of bed when you don't feel like it. It is your northern star, your guiding principle, your greater purpose. Write it down, at first it may seem like a jumble of words, but spend a little time refining it into one clear sentence. Put it somewhere you can see it and read it every day. It may change over time and that's ok. When you have focus and intention on your big WHY, your brain will figure out a way to make it happen.

I recently calculated that it takes a minimum of 2,500 euro each month to keep my home ticking over, without needing to squeeze out the tea bags. I decided that by doubling that number, it would make me feel more relaxed and by trebling that number, it would bring a greater sense of freedom. By the way, you can never feel too free.

For me, financial freedom is more than just money coming in; it focuses on *how* that money comes in. I would prefer that money to come from unearned sources rather than earned sources.

Earned income comes from my physical labour. It means I have to get out of bed, do my hair, wear something other than my pyjamas, make myself look presentable and hurl myself out the door to do some work.

There are two ways to make money. You can work for your money or you can put your money to work for you.

Unearned or passive income comes from multiple alternative sources instead of paid employment. The possibilities for passive income are infinite. Think laterally, think creatively – don't box yourself in here as it will have a direct impact on your ability to earn that passive income.

Some examples could include:

- Rental income
- Royalty income
- Investment income
- Dividends
- Multi-level marketing income from your downline
- Online courses
- Membership websites
- Affiliate income

The list goes on and on.

Robert Kiyosaki, author of the *Rich Dad Poor Dad* series, coined the phrase "the cash flow quadrant".

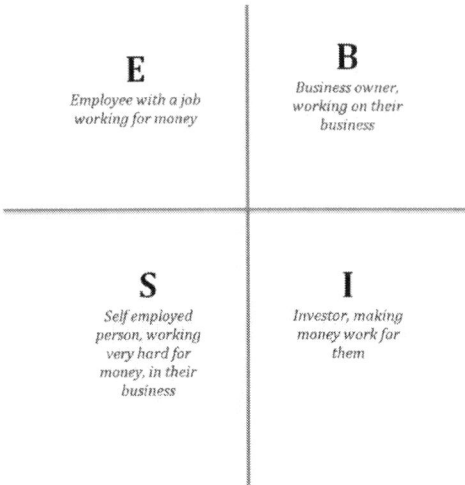

E *Employee with a job working for money*	**B** *Business owner, working on their business*
S *Self employed person, working very hard for money, in their business*	**I** *Investor, making money work for them*

Most people spend all their time on the left-hand side of the square, which is reserved for employees and the self-employed. Unfortunately, self-employed people often end up overworked and underpaid, which is what they were trying to avoid when they left their jobs to become self-employed.

Self-employed people work in their businesses and are often so busy doing the work, that they lose sight of why they started on this path initially.

The magic exists on the right-hand side of the square.

You can become a business owner by buying into a business you have no clue about so that you are forced to hire a manager. In this situation, you keep an eye on the bottom line and work *on* the business, not in it.

The investor does not care if he gets out of bed or not. The investor goes to sleep every night knowing that money will flow in regardless.

It does not have to be a case of choosing one or the other option. You could even maintain a presence in all four squares if you choose. However, it can take time to transition from one square to the next and even from one side of the square to the other. Incremental changes can make a big impact, so start small, but make sure you start. Figure out where you are now and where you want to go.

How I Started in Peer-to-Peer Lending

I love watching *Dragon's Den* and *The Apprentice*. I used to imagine myself as an investor listening to amazing stories of creativity and entrepreneurship, making an offer in return for a share of that person's business. However, on the other side of that dream was the sense that money was a huge obstacle for me. I was not sitting on a pile of cash and, even if I was, what on earth do I know about business?

Despite these niggling feelings, I decided that this was something I wanted to do in some shape or form. So, I wrote it down in my journal. By setting my intention, writing it down, and letting go of how it might occur, I had set myself up for success and before long an opportunity presented itself to me. A few months later, two interesting events occurred.

I was at a business-networking event and I heard an Irish man speak about peer-to-peer lending. The same week, I watched a documentary about Dave Fishwick, from Burley, in the UK, and his story of *The Bank of Dave*. Through hearing his story, I realised that I could be a "dragon"! I could support an Irish business and I could reap the rewards of being an investor but with a much smaller stake. This was my opportunity to start moving myself toward the right-hand side of Kiyosaki's cash flow quadrant.

Personally, I like the idea of "try before you buy". I like to try clothes on at home before taking the tags off. I like to taste new food before committing to a whole dish. I like to test drive different cars to find the one I want. It is possible, even easy, to open a peer-to-peer lending account with a small amount of money so that you can try it out.

The idea of making a financial investment used to strike fear into my heart. I would stress out that I had to invest a huge lump sum – for me, huge was anything over 1,000 euro. I would have to hand it over to someone; either the bank or the faceless man in a suit, and then worry for years about whether my money had been invested correctly and if I would ever see it again.

Despite my expertise as a financial adviser and my own personal journey as an investor, financial investments still make me slightly nervous. Luckily, this nervous feeling now comes more from a place of excitement than anxiety. Every transaction carries risk. However, there is a big difference between taking risk and being risky.

Risk

Risk is calculated, understood and accepted. It suggests that the client has done the research, worked out the ups and downs and knows what they are getting into. They understand and accept the fees and charges, know what their strategy is and know how to get out when they want to. The client also understands the time frame involved and is satisfied that the investment aligns with their values.

Risky is something very different, it involves throwing caution to the wind. Risky is running across a busy road without looking, it is jumping without a parachute, playing a one-armed bandit at a casino, playing the lottery, or investing in a business you know nothing about from an unscrupulous source, like a stranger in a bar.

Let's look at how banks manage risk.

Banking in its simplest form comes down to the 3-6-3 rule.

Banks accept money from you as savings, put it on deposit and offer you, the customer, 3% interest in return.

They, then, take your money and lend it out at 6% interest. Before the bank lends the money, they will first make sure they have the money to lend and then they make sure that the person borrowing the money has the ability to pay it back. This is one of the storylines in the classic film *It's a Wonderful Life*.

The bank makes money on the bit in the middle which is the difference between what they offer you as interest and what they earn by lending it out. The technical term for the "bit in the middle" is arbitrage or the interest rate spread. This concept has been around since 2,000 B.C.

It can help to think of money as a product. The bank buys stock for 3 units and sells it for 6 units. This means that they make a profit of 3 units. When the system is this easy, effortless, and straightforward, it's no wonder bank managers can rush off and play golf at 3 pm on a Friday afternoon!

What if we turned this around and you, the customer, became the lender?

That's what peer-to-peer lending, also known as P2P lending, is all about. You, as an individual, get to lend your money to businesses and make a profit on the bit in the middle.

Sounds simple? That's because it is!

Jonathan Swift, the famous Irish author of *Gulliver's Travels*, lent money to Irish farmers via the Irish Loan Fund in 1727 and, occasionally, without charging interest. This system has stood the test of time and is still around because it works. I'm not a fan of new-fangled anything.

How Peer-to-Peer Lending Works

To make life easier and to keep your money secure, all of the lending and borrowing is done through regulated and registered third parties. Someone has to do the heavy lifting. Think of it as a dating agency for lenders and borrowers. You have money to lend and want to find someone suitable, reliable, trustworthy, and preferably, a non-smoker to lend it to. You don't really have the time, mental energy, or patience to hunt for this person yourself, so simply hire someone to do the research. That's where the peer-to-peer lending company come in. They pair lenders with borrowers.

Let's say I have a business and I would like some working capital to enable it to grow. I could empty my piggy bank, take out a bank loan, apply for a grant, hassle family members, buy a lottery ticket, hope for the best, or approach a peer-to-peer lending company.

When a business owner approaches the peer-to-peer lending company, they will be asked lots of questions about the business, they need to provide their business plan and a credit and risk score will be calculated for them. If their proposal looks good, the business will be put forward to lenders; individuals like you and me, who want to lend money and make a good return. The lenders can then read a short summary of the business, find out what the money will be used for and how long they intend to borrow for. These types of loans are usually short-term; anything between 12 months to 36 months.

When the lender has satisfied themselves that the business involved is one they would like to back, they can make an offer of an amount of money and an interest rate. The lender can usually dictate the interest rate within a range of approximately 0% to 15%. It's like bidding at an auction but less stressful. At the end of the bidding process, which normally lasts a few weeks, the business looking to borrow the money can accept or decline the loan. The full amount of the loan is made up of multiple offers from multiple lenders at different rates of interest. Once the loan has been drawn down, the borrower starts to repay it the following month and that's where the real magic happens.

The borrowers pay the loan back with interest and that's how the peer-to-peer company and you, the lender, make money. As a lender, you see your investment grow in front of your eyes as repayments are made each month. The repayments don't go into your bank account or your wallet. Instead, they go back into your lender account, which is held in escrow so that you can take it out, go mad, and spend it, sit on it or lend it out again to someone else. Escrow is an account that does not officially belong to anyone so there is no real benefit for the peer-to-peer lending business to sit on your money. Lather, rinse, and repeat.

The peer-to-peer company usually takes a percentage of the interest and the rest of the profits go to the lender. The peer-to-peer company takes care of the research, collects the money, distributes the repayments, problem solves if something goes wrong, chases late payments, and pursues loans that go into default. Yes, this can happen, it's life, but business loans are usually more secure, particularly when there is a director's guarantee in place.

Even if a loan is late being paid back to you, or worse, does not get paid back, the rate of return is still more than if you had stashed your money under the bed or left it on deposit. That said, the rate of loans that are not paid back is generally low.

The Advantages of Peer-to-Peer Lending

It's easy

You can manage it yourself if you want to or set up automatic bids for loans.

You can usually decide the rate of interest. I indicated earlier that loans start at 0%. From a business perspective, it makes no sense to lend money for no return. However, I also believe that the more one has, the more one can give. Personally, I keep space to allow at least one loan at 0%. This is like a charitable donation, but the upside is that I get my money back, knowing that I have helped someone else along the way. I might offer this type of loan to a business, cause that matters to me, or a non-profit.

You get email notifications to let you know how much has been repaid and from whom. I love this part, I have a "wealthy woman" swagger every time I get a loan repayment. My repayments have been as small as 50c up to a few hundred euro depending on how big the original loan was.

You can physically see your money growing in front of your eyes. You can also log in and check how your loans are doing at any time.

In Ireland, peer-to-peer lending is reasonably tax-efficient. As of the date of writing, you can earn up to 1,270 euro free of capital gains tax per year. If I can earn something tax-free, I'm usually first in the queue! Compare this with interest rates for your money on deposit. If you put your money in the bank, they will say thank you very much and offer you a low rate of interest that also attracts a deposit tax at the end of the year.

Someone else does the heavy lifting

You can start with small amounts in your lender account and small loans as you build your confidence with the system.

You are supporting your own economy and a local business.

Everything is done in one currency, so you don't end up playing the Foreign Exchange game that no one knows the rules to.

You can decide who to lend to and how much to lend. Warren Buffet, one of the world's most successful investors, has a simple philosophy -*Invest in businesses you understand.*

Buffet invested in Gillette Razors because he was able to imagine men, like him, getting up every morning, and shaving. He did not understand technology, so he avoided businesses in this area and, as a result, managed to avoid the dot-com bubble.

You can lend at a low rate of interest if you want. People have different reasons for wanting to do this. Whatever your reasons, it's nice to know that you can do it.

How awesome does it feel to say, "pull up a seat and let me tell you about my self-directed investment portfolio"?

You get to learn the strategies and language of wealthy people

Sometimes there are incentives to lend money to a particular business or you might get an exclusive invitation to an event. I've been invited to a few exclusive business launches through peer-to-peer lending.

The online platform allows you to manage things yourself from anywhere that has an Internet connection.

The average annual return is about 9%, which is not too shabby compared with deposit interest rates.

You can choose from a wide range of businesses to lend to. You can think like Warren Buffet and choose a business that you understand or dip your toe in the water with new and emerging technology companies. The choice is entirely yours.

You can bypass the mainstream banks

You get first-hand information on which business sectors are expanding, who is doing what, and if you are in business yourself, you could possibly even keep an eye on your competitors. Use this information ethically and honestly. It's not insider trading on Wall Street.

The Downsides of Peer-to-Peer Lending

It takes a bit of work. You can do as much or as little as you want.

The online platforms can seem a bit complicated at first. Most new activities take a bit of getting used to, but most things are "figurableoutable". If you're really stuck, you can always pick up the telephone and ask for help.

Your loan might not be repaid if the business falls apart. However, before a loan becomes visible to lenders, the business has to be put through the wringer to prove that it can be repaid. So, while there is a chance that the loan won't be repaid, it doesn't happen all that often. We're back to the concept of risk.

You don't have access to your money if you lend it out

It is best to work with amounts of money that you do not need access to in the next couple of years. Most of the loans are a maximum of 36 months – 3 years. If you really needed your money back, you simply take your money out as the loans are repaid and don't lend it out again.

There are fees and charges

Everyone needs to get paid. As long as you understand the charges, accept them and feel you are getting value for money, that's ok.

You will need to declare any profits on your tax return

Tax is not automatically deducted at source like a paycheque. This can be enough to turn some people off, but remember, wealthy people hire accountants and do tax returns. If you want to be wealthy, you will need to start thinking like a wealthy person.

You bypass the mainstream banks

Yes, this was on the list of advantages. Whether you see this as a pro or a con is up to you.

Ready, Steady, Go!

If you are ready to start your journey in peer-to-peer lending, then let's make it happen. If you are serious about taking control of your own financial freedom, take action. The amount of money does not matter, the action does. There is power in momentum.

Step 1

Find a peer-to-peer lending business in your country or currency.

Make sure that they are regulated in line with the laws of your country.

Step 2

Create an account. You must be over 18 years of age and will have to upload photo ID, proof of address and your social security number as a minimum security requirement. Decide how much you are willing to invest to get started. Pick an amount that you are comfortable with until you find your feet. You can always add more later.

Step 3

Add money to your account. It's like adding money to a prepaid credit card.

Start lending. Pick a business that you like. Make an offer and then wait for it to be accepted.

Step 4

Do the happy dance when you get your first repayment.

Reinvest your money and watch it grow.

Celebrate that you have taken one powerful step toward securing your financial freedom.

Peer-to-peer lending is a flexible way for individuals to flex their investing muscles in a way that suits them. It allows you to support local businesses that are doing good work and who may not get the financial support they need to grow from traditional lending institutions. You have power when you sign up to peer-to-peer lending, power to transform your financial future, but also to support local business in securing theirs too.

Remember that you can start small, take your time, and let your own gut guide your decisions. There is no need to invest in a business which doesn't make sense to you, do your research and choose the businesses to invest in which resonate with you. Try to have fun with it. Yes, it's your money and that is serious, but it can be an enjoyable process too. Let yourself enjoy it.

Aoife Gaffney

About the author

Aoife Gaffney MSc (Hons) BSc (Open) LIB QFA CMC, also known as Prudence Moneypenny, CEO and Founder of Prudence Moneypenny Coaching

Prudence Moneypenny is the pen name of Aoife Gaffney. She is Ireland's only Certified Money Coach and money mindset mentor. She is also an accredited life coach.

She lives in Kildare with her son, her books, and her collection of odd socks.

She is in her fourth decade. She is an entrepreneur, a blogger, and a bargain hunter. She is the self-professed queen of money makeovers, a qualified financial adviser, with many years' experience in financial education, debt destruction and wealth building. She offers money mindset mentoring and coaching rather than financial advice.

She is also an eternal student, mediocre cook, NLP practitioner and aspiring gardener. She is self-employed by choice, with sporadic income (not by choice) however, by following her own advice; she lives absolutely debt free.

It is hard to be afraid of something you laugh at. Managing your money can be scary. Prudence makes it easy. She shares her financial mistakes and laughs at them. Her mantra is "master your mind, master your money".

She has two addictions - really good coffee and decent broadband.

When she is not writing, cleaning, renovating her house or organising her sock drawer, she usually has her head in a book or glued to her Kindle. She loves spending time with her family although they often just see the back of her head if she is engrossed in a project.

Join her and other like-minded people in discussing how to live a financially free life by heading over to her Facebook group at:
https://www.facebook.com/groups/prudencemoneypenny
or get the inside exclusive inside scoop at :
https://www.patreon.com/prudencemoneypenny

Buy to Let Property

The direct purchase of real estate generally for the purpose of letting out to generate an income and ideally an increase in the capital value. The old cliché of location, location, location is very important here and often determines the demand for a property due to employment, facilities and amenities in an area. In the right locations supply tends to be restricted due to land being a limited commodity and, therefore, if there is a strong demand then prices tend to increase. Similar to shares, the return tends to 6-8% per annum but the big differentiating factor with property is the ability for finance over the long term at low interest rates and that lenders have no ability to call in the loan until the end of the period.

Why Property?

You may be thinking that property investment is only for people with money or wealthy fat cat landlords and I don't blame you as that is what I thought before getting involved. This chapter of *Financial Freedom Explained* will provide a summary of how the average "mum and dad" investor which we define as a person or couple living the average UK family life that are generally between the ages of 30 to 50, can achieve success using this asset class. If you're interested in replacing your employment income with passive income generating from your investments with little effort from you, the holy grail of investing, then Property Investment is for you.

Returns

The returns generated from leveraged buy to let property over the past 20 years have been quite incredible. The average return on funds invested in a buy to let with 75% leverage over 20 years to 2013 was 16.1% per annum. Which greatly exceeds the returns generated by other popular investment asset classes. A strong contributing factor to these returns and the major advantage the property holds is the ability to borrow money at high loan to value rate, low interest rates and for long periods of time without taking too much risk. To borrow to invest in shares, there is quite a bit of risk as, generally, the highest loan to value is approximately 60% (40% of your own cash invested), rates at the time of writing range up from 6% and if the value of your shares fall below an accepted level then you either must sell or contribute more funds. This often results in people selling at the worst possible time and losing money simply because market sentiment is low. This being said, even as a cash purchase, property has outperformed the FTSE All Share index consistently.

It's important to note that without the prudent use of investment debt it is very difficult for the vast majority of people to achieve their lifestyle and financial goals. Even if they saved most of their income they still would not have enough funds to retire and passively generate the income that they need. So it is important to assess the best use of your resources and make investments that not only fit with your risk vs reward profile, but also align with your target timeframe and current resources.

Since 1926, house prices in the UK have, on average, more than quadrupled every 20 years. Compared with the share market, the FTSE 100 is lower today than it was in 1999.

Income

The current average rental yield available on UK property is approximately 5%. This means that you are able to achieve approximately £1 per £10,000 investment per week. E.g. a £100,000 property will rent for approximately £100 a week. The average growth in rental yield has been 4.2% per annum which is versus a historical inflation rate of 2% which means that rents are growing at a much faster rate than people's incomes. Therefore as opposed to many other investment types, at current interest rates of 2-3% it actually makes sense to borrow for income. This is due to the yield being higher than the cost of borrowing which accelerates your returns. For example a property that is yielding 7% (2% higher than the UK average but very achievable in the right areas) a 75% mortgage will often provide a return on cash invested up 12-15% per annum after all expenses and excluding any potential growth. Rental demand and growth is very much determined by demand and therefore so long as you invest in the right areas with strong reasons for people to want to live there, then you can have confidence in rental demand regardless of the state of the economy.

Comparing this to shares, the average dividend form the FTSE 100 is 4.2% and interest rates are 6%+. Given the interest rate is higher than the yield, it doesn't make any sense to borrow to invest in shares if your main goal is to generate income. Even if you invested in higher yielding types of shares where the yield was 6%+, the gap would be minimal and therefore the cash flow wouldn't be far above neutral. Average dividend growth in the FTSE 100 has been 3% but the risk with dividends is that they can drop at the whim of management or if the company or market isn't performing well.

Stability, Volatility and Risk

Property tends to be a more stable and reliable investment when compared to other investment options. During the financial crisis of 2008, UK property values fell by 8%. In the same year, the FTSE All Share Index fell by 31%.

Property is a tangible asset that so long as it is structural stable cannot disappear and will therefore retain some value even in bad economic times. Vice-versa even the biggest publicly listed companies can go bust and share values can go to zero.

Furthermore, in an economic crisis, assuming your property is in the right location, then you can have confidence that it will still rent and provide an income even in bad times. In fact, rents often increase in an economic downturn because there is less funding in the market and more rental pressure especially in high employment areas. This is as opposed to shares, where both prices and dividends tend to drop, companies can't pay dividends if they aren't making a profit.

Reinvesting And Liquidity

Net cash flow from property can be applied to paying down the debt which will enable to investor to reduce the loan to value ratio quicker and as the property grows in value you can potentially re-mortgage to reinvest further properties sooner.

Property is generally a high value asset and is often the most expensive purchase that people will ever make. Given properties larger purchase price, it requires the application of large sums of money to each investment, some perceive this as a downside of the asset class. A deposit needs to be saved which is most often in the tens of thousands. However, if buying the right properties in the right areas, vague I know but we will cover this more later, selling your property can be quick and easy.

Intro to Property

The Basics

The average income in the UK for a full-time employee is £27,123 which, based upon a 5% net yield, would require an investable asset base of £542,640. Therefore, without investing the average employee would need to save all of their income over 20 years or half their income over 40 years to get there and even then the value of their money will be eroded by inflation. So it stands to reason that without investing it will be very difficult to achieve your retirement goals.

Passive income is income generated from investments in a way that require little to no time from the investor. Often this style of investing is called "arm chair" investing which is the opposite of being hands on and going out to fix the toilets of your properties every weekend. This is generally the strategy followed by property owners that consider themselves investors rather than landlords. Investors generally view property as being a box that generates money, as opposed to an ongoing project.

Debt Free Property is property bought with cash as opposed to taking a mortgage. This is the most conservative way to buy property as there is no risk of interest rates rising or meeting mortgage repayments if your property is empty.

Leveraged property is property bought with a mortgage. The standard buy to let mortgage loan to value in the UK is 75% which means that a 25% deposit is required to purchase. Leveraged property gives the ability to generate returns on a higher value asset or assets than if you were a cash buyer there are risks and therefore can accelerate returns. This is of course risky because if the value of the property falls it can also accelerate losses as well as the risks of interest rates rising and meeting mortgage repayments.

Positive Cash Flow Property is property that generates more income than all costs required to maintain the property such as mortgage repayments, lettings and management, services charges and ground rent as well as maintenance. For example, a property that rents for £1,000 per month and has £700 per month of expenses is £300 per month cash flow positive. Many investors aim for cash flow positive properties as the total Buy to let mortgages are the mortgages available for properties that are bought for the purpose of renting to a tenant. These mortgages first became available in the UK in 1996 when buy to let became very popular due to the strong returns available. Historically interest rates have been higher than residential mortgages. However that has changed in recent years with the increase in competition in lending, there are now many buy to let mortgage products available at similar rates to residential mortgages. At the time of writing (September 2016) 75% buy to let mortgage rate are available at interest rates of less than 2%.

Interest rates are the cost of borrowing and are referred to in percentage terms which is the amount that you pay the lender as a proportion of the amount you've borrowed. For example, if you borrow £100,000 at an interest rate of 3% then your yearly interest repayment is £3,000. This is if the loan repayments are on an interest only basis whereas with principal and interest loans there is also a repayment portion over and above the interest repayments. Most buy to let mortgage are interest only but some investors choose to take principle and interest mortgages especially if they no longer have any personal debt (e.g. their home loan).

Tax on Buy to Let Properties, the NET (income after expenses) income generated from property investment is taxable and forms part of your yearly income for tax purposes. There are various tax strategies and ways of structuring an investment that is suitable for your situation which is an area worth getting advice on if you're an active investor or planning to invest.

Expenses are tax deductible. Currently all expenses incurred in running and maintaining a property investment are tax deductible against the income generated. There are impending changes to this rule which mean that by 2020 mortgage interest will no longer be deductible but a tax credit will be given at the basic rate of tax of 20%. This means that if you earn less than £45,000 including property income then the changes won't affect you. If you earn more than £45,000 your property investments will be less tax efficient and you should seek advice on any potential solutions.

Returns from property are given in the form of income and/or capital growth. Cash flow is the rental income minus expenses and capital growth is the increase in the property value over time. Some investors prefer one or the other depending on what they are hoping to achieve from their investment.

The returns

In a report titled *"Buy To Let Comes Of Age"* which was commissioned by Paragon Mortgages and conducted by Wrigglesworth as research house, it was determined that the average buy to let property that was purchased with cash generated returns of 9.7% per annum after all expenses and the same property with a 75% buy to let mortgage generated returns of 16.3% per annum over 18 years up to 2013. That is versus 6.8% from the FTSE all shares index and 4% from cash.

What are your investment options? - Investing 101

When it comes to investing, you have three broad options which are; Interest bearing investments, Shares and Property. Other investments such as commodities and fine wine etc don't generate an income and are therefore more of a speculation on their potential for an increase in value rather than an investment. Which one is right for you? Well it very much depends.

Interest bearing investments

This type of investment includes cash in the bank, term deposits, ISAs and any other type of investment where you invest your funds and receive a fixed or variable cash flow return without the chance of the capital value of your investment increasing or decreasing other than with inflation. You can get your initial funds back at some point in the future with interest. In general, historical returns tend to be approximately 2-4% per annum.

Shares

When investing in shares you are buying a portion of ownership in a company. There are many different ways to determine which companies you should invest in such as fundamentals, qualitative, value; analysis or simply guessing and hoping for the best and so on which are outside the scope of this book. However mostly it is based upon optimism with regards to the prospect of that company. Often such companies will have a historical return that is made up of capital appreciation (or depreciation) and dividends which is the yearly income provided through the share of profits. In general, historical returns tend to be approximately 6-8% per annum but vary greatly across different sectors and types of companies.

Property

The direct purchase of real estate generally for the purpose of letting out to generate an income and ideally an increase in the capital value. The old cliché of location, location, location is very important here and often determines the demand for a property due to employment, facilities and amenities in an area. In the right locations supply tends to be restricted due to land being a limited commodity and therefore if there is a strong demand then prices tend to increase. Similar to shares, the return tends to 6-8% per annum but the big differentiating factor with property is the ability for finance over the long term at low interest rates and that lenders have no ability to call in the loan until the end of the period.

Should you borrow to invest?

When it comes to making an investment, you must decide whether your investment will be solely cash or whether you will leverage your cash to make a larger investment. Taking on debt to invest can be higher risk but not taking debt can put you at risk of not meeting your goals and under-utilising your money. Unfortunately, most people struggle to save sufficient funds over their working life to be able to provide for retirement so the prudent use of investment debt is in many cases essential to reach set goals.

If you're investing in interest bearing investments, then, in most cases, borrowing doesn't make any sense. This is because the cost of borrowing will outweigh the return and hence defeat the purpose.

When investing in shares, you can borrow to invest with what is called a margin loan. Margin loans work on the basis that your lending can only be a certain percentage of your portfolio value. The risk here is if the value of your shares falls and therefore the loan percentage increases then you can be forced to sell at the worst time or add more money in a falling market. Interest rates tend to high (6%+ at the time of writing in early 2017) and maximum loan to values of 60%. So borrowing to invest in shares is high risk and high cost - meaning the return you need to generate must be higher to make it worthwhile.

Property is the third option, which enables you to borrow at low interest rates of 2-3% at the time of writing, for the long term 20 years plus, with no ability for recall and at loan to value rates of 75%+. So low risk, low cost and hence an average return can actually result in a great return on the cash invested given the multiplying factors that debt provides. E.g. £25,000 invested in a £100,000 property; just a 5% increase in value which is less than the historical average is a 20% return on your £25,000 of £5,000. Assuming your rental yield is sufficiently higher than the interest rate and costs then you can also add net income. This is the beauty of leveraged property, fairly average returns on the overall value result in great returns on your cash applied. Add to this the ability to re-mortgage to invest further when you build equity through price growth and pay down debt with the income and you have a strong strategy for building an investable asset base over the long term.

The R.E.T.I.R.E. Investment Journey

I.   Ready to get started

At this stage of your life you are just starting to think about investing. For most this is between the ages of 25 and 35 but don't worry of you are outside this bracket as many successful people started earlier or later than this. This is the beginning of financial awareness. It is the time when you realise that working long hours to earn more money but then spend it all or not do anything useful with it isn't enough. You want to be able to utilise your money and you want to learn how to do that. Congratulations this is the first step in a long process.

II.   Education

In this stage research and education is of utmost importance, you need to build your knowledge base and ideally seek the advice of a trusted advisor to assist you to get started on the right path. This is essentially the cornerstone of your investment journey as often the first investment will either give you the confidence to keep going or you'll get your fingers burnt which could affect your progression. Do your research but try not to self-diagnose; this is comparable to going online and looking up why you have a sore throat. Often you will end up thinking you have a life-threatening disease when in fact you just have a cold. Seeking advice on what is right for your situation and what you are trying to achieve is akin to going to the doctor. This doesn't mean that you shouldn't do your own research but there is a lot of conflicting information out there that can often result in paralysis by analysis. You can spend far too much time going around in circles but remember that until you've invested you haven't actually achieved anything so far as improving your financial situation.

III.   Testing the Water

Starting with a low risk investment that you are very confident in and one that provides steady returns is advisable at this stage. All too often I see first time investors trying to be too creative to create "fast equity" which they've often heard about at a "get rich quick seminar" or similar event and fortunately or unfortunately such investments tend to be high risk. They often profess unachievable returns or in some cases are just non-existent solely for the purpose of selling a seminar or training course. My advice is to start small and low risk and build from there as your confidence and wealth - and therefore your ability to weather a loss - builds.

IV.   Investing Further

In this stage, you've already made your first investment and hopefully that went well. You're now looking to build an asset base and move closer toward your long-term goal. You may start to make larger investments or take on more creative projects as your confidence and wealth builds. Don't get carried away and start to think that you're an expert (unless you are), an over-confident investor is often an unwise investor. So don't just jump into things. Maintain in-depth research and due diligence at every turn to ensure you don't get burnt or make the wrong decision for your situation. This phase should focus on capital growth investments, whilst income is important to support costs when you're building an asset base, you are much more likely to reach your goal sooner through growth than through income. A quick example below;

A £50,000 investment into a 10% NET yielding asset (the upper end of what is achievable) will give you £5,000 per annum. If it doesn't grow in value, then £5,000 is all you will ever get in a year.

The same £50,000 invested into a £200,000 property with 75% leverage that doubles in value in 10 years means that the £50,000 is now worth £250,000. Do that a few times and you will be much more likely to achieve the income you want in the subsequent phases of your investment journey.

This can be likened to growing and squeezing an orange; when you have a small orange, there isn't much point in picking and squeezing it because you're unlikely to get much juice. When that orange has grown big and juicy then is the time to squeeze. The orange is your asset base and the juice is cash flow.

Your investments should be chosen accordingly; depending on the type of return that is most suitable for your stage of the investment journey.

V.   Retirement Transitioning

This phase is when you've reached the required asset base to generate the income that you require. However often the investments you've made have been capital growth focussed and may not be generating you sufficient income. This is a common shift to which there are a few solutions; you could sell up and completely shift into income focussed investments or you could liquidate part of your portfolio to accommodate the shift. The answer will differ depending on your situation but it is important to remain commercially minded and not get attached to investments regardless of how well they've performed if they are not generating the right type of income for you.

A family friend recently inherited a reasonable sum and invested in ten factories in a regional town of the UK. Aside from being slightly offended that he didn't ask me for investment advice on what he should do with the money, I thought he was crazy, what could 10 factories in a small town have going for them as an investment? They're never going to grow in value and surely there isn't that much demand from tenants, is what I thought. I asked him why he did it and his response was that he had pre-leased them for 20 years at a 10%+ yield and given he is 60 years of age, he couldn't care less about growth as the kids can worry about that. Little did I know that my family friend clearly understood that he had the asset base required to generate the income that he needed and wasn't worried about the exit strategy or growth as that would be beyond his timeframe of caring. Not so crazy!

VI.   Easy Retirement

If the previous phases have been done right, then this phase is about enjoying the fruits of your labour. Whatever your goals were they should now be achieved and you are able to enjoy life and appreciate the work that you put into getting you here. Now of course you may need to tweak things here and there based upon economic or legislative changes but ideally they can be looked after by someone else.

Value of advice

When you're sick you go to the doctor, to do your taxes you go to an accountant, when investing in property you should seek advice. Property is often the largest purchase you will ever make with the current average property price of circa £250,000. Most people don't spend that sort of money every day and it therefore shouldn't be taken lightly. Despite this, property investment tends to be a very do it yourself activity which for me is difficult to understand. I would like to think that my level of understanding of property and investments is slightly higher than your average person through years advising others and over a decade of study. But I would not make such a large decision without seeking the advice of others who know what they are talking about and are independent in their advice. We as humans are emotional creatures and I believe that I've been saved from many bad decisions simply by using a trusted advisor as a sounding board which allowed me to see reason.

Ensure that, when seeking advice, you meet with a company that is independent and not just selling products or investments. I am a strong believer that prescription without diagnosis is malpractice and by this, I mean you need to seek the advice of a company or person who takes the time to very clearly understand your situation, goals and preference prior to providing advice. Avoid those that advertise specific investment options or products as more often than not, that is what you are going to end up with.

Also, be wary of those that try to convince you of investment options that are completely outside your comfort zone. It really doesn't matter how much sense an investment makes on a spreadsheet, if you're not comfortable with it, and you're going to lie awake at night worrying about it, then it isn't right for you.

Although some advisors will show you fancy graphs and stats to back up their advice, a man convinced against his will is of the same opinion still. So don't let the hype fool you into something you're not ok with.

The property industry unfortunately tends to be very sales focussed which means that, when it comes to making a purchase, you are often dealing with a salesperson in the form of an estate agent or property marketer. The difference between sales and advice is that in the right circumstances, advice focusses on benefits whereas sales focussed on features. When dealing with an estate agent they will tell you how great the property is because it has a south west facing garden and a period fireplace but do those things really matter? In some cases, they do if that is what your target market wants. But how does that relate to you? That's where advice becomes very useful as good advice focusses on benefits. Benefits being what the property can do for you and how it relates to you. Another way of putting it is the outcomes rather than the offering.

Paul A Mahoney

About the author

The author of this chapter is Paul Mahoney who has over a decade of experience in financial planning and property investment. His formal qualifications include a bachelor of business majoring in Financial Planning, a diploma of financial services, a certificate in mortgage advice and practice (Cemap) and he has studied the better part of an executive MBA.

He started his career in Australia as a project manager in large scale developments across NSW and QLD where he gained a strong understanding of property development. A few years later he moved into financial services with Spring Financial Group and due to his ability to relate to clients and help them achieve financial success, he quickly progressed to executive management with Spring which is now publicly listed on the Australian stock exchange.

Paul is now the Founder and Managing Director at Nova Financial, the multi award winning, independent finance and property advisory company with offices in London, Manchester & Birmingham. Nova Financials' new approach to advice and values reflect Paul's, with regards to providing objective advice and helping people to achieve financial freedom through focussing on the individual's goals and preferences rather than just selling products or investments.

Nova is the industry leader in property advice as they are dedicated to helping their clients achieve financial freedom through what they believe to be the most stable and reliable investment asset class available, Property. Paul is a recognised property and finance expert, commentator, landlord and key note speaker. He delivers 20-30 seminars and talks a year throughout the UK and overseas, he is also commonly featured in the media in leading publications and on leading property and finance television shows.

Paul and his team at Nova can assist investors of all levels of experience and ability to quantify and achieve their financial and lifestyle goals. Feel free to get in touch at www.nova.financial, 0203 8000 600 or info@nova.financial .

Understanding Your Relationship with Money

Working with money and planning a successful financial future are not native abilities we are born with. These are skills we must learn, or risk feeling inadequate to navigate our financial destiny. Unfortunately, few of us were taught these skills either in our families or in school, which is why I chose my profession as Money Coach. A great footballer has a coach, and coupled with hours of training becomes the pro. A great graphic designer takes a graphic design course, studies different programmes and techniques to achieve their skill. It is the same with finance – no one was born a financial genius.

Achieving financial success, however, is only 20 percent about learning practical money skills. The remaining 80 per cent is about understanding your emotions and behaviours relative to money. Your money patterns and mindset are the biggest players when it comes to achieving financial freedom or wealth.

Money plays a huge part in our lives. It is essential, not optional. We hope and dream of having plenty of money. We fear not having enough money. Money very often defines who we are. We make huge life decisions based on money – marriage, divorce, education, and career. Developing an emotional connection with money is inevitable. If we are to set ourselves up for success with money, we must learn to understand how the society we live in creates dysfunctional expectations about money and how these impact us as individuals.

As a money coach, I see clients who are keen to achieve financial freedom, but just can't seem to "make it." Stories unfold of detailed plans to reach financial freedom, only to find them failing at the first hurdle. This might be through an argument with a partner or simply veering off plan believing that a shinier object somewhere else will give a greater return. Other tales reveal our fear and mistrust of investing in anything other than a safe, very low interest account which will never fund our longer-term needs or financial plans. Many more have no plan at all, coupled with a fear or unease of making one. Whatever the story, there is always an underlying emotion or behaviour that eludes us.

I often ask my clients, "If money was your lover, how would you describe your relationship with it? Would it be warm and close? Do you just about tolerate each other? Or, are you currently living apart?" While the responses vary, they generally tell me that it would be a relationship they consider far from ideal.

Many of us live with fear, greed, anxiety, and shame around money, making little, if any attempt to understand why we have these feelings or where they came from. Compounding these feelings is the fact that we choose to keep them to ourselves, secretly believing that we are the only ones that feel this way. But this is far from true. Money is one of the few taboo subjects left, but whilst we stay silent, the repressed negative feelings and beliefs we have about money, keep us entrapped and unable to make better choices and create the lives we dream of, but cannot seem to actualize.

So how did our relationship with money end up this way? Largely, these patterns become hard-wired at an early age, subconsciously influenced by our family and those around us. Taking the time to focus and understand our money behaviours and emotions allows us to fill in the blanks and become aware of the patterns we acquired when we were merely a child. Without this awareness, we remain blind to these patterns and most of us will continue to struggle without knowing why. If we are willing to dive deeper, by looking at the origin of those patterns and behaviours, we can begin to understand and heal our relationship with money in a relatively short period of time.

Every person I have worked with, who chooses to discover and understand their true relationship with money, has been able to find a better and easier way to hop onto and follow the path to financial freedom. Indeed, if we are to live a balanced healthy life in both mind, body and spirit then a harmonious relationship with money is near, if not top, of the list.

Our relationship with money is shaped by our 'money story'. This begins with our first money experience. It may be being given a shiny coin for being 'good' by a grandparent. It may be anxiously watching a coin, that was meant for a treat, roll down a dirty drain. Everybody's story is different. Some have dramatic stories that take twists and turns like an adventure movie. Many harbour a story of shame and embarrassment, which they prefer not to share. Others decide to play the opposing role in their adult life money story, whilst others continue the theme, keeping the story rolling as an ongoing legacy.

It is critical that you understand your story – be able to see it objectively and consciously. To do that ask yourself:

- What is your earliest memory of money?
- What was the experience like?
- How did that experience affect you?

Ask these questions for as many money experiences and observations that you have had throughout your life that you can recall. Think of the key people in your story and how significant they were. What messages, patterns or behaviours related to money did you learn from them? I suggest you write your money story down. You can then read it back taking a helicopter view and gain new perspective.

Largely, the beliefs we create around money are formed between the ages of two and twelve years old. During the remainder of our formative years, they have time to calcify and become hardwired in the brain. By adulthood, some will be so deep that we do not even recognise that they are there.

We rely on parents, grandparents, and siblings to be our role models. Like a sponge, we absorb what they do and say. We look to their knowledge to teach us how to be. But what are we taught? What do we see? And how does this affect our relationship with money in later life?

If we grow up hearing arguments over spending, this can frighten us as children. It may cause us to form the negative beliefs that spending money causes arguments, or that money is a problem best avoided. Watching our parents struggle with money may impact our desire to manage our own finances – as doing so means frustration and anger. Receiving presents instead of love or affection may inspire feelings of entitlement. Shopping trips presented as entertainment may well encourage overspending and a careless attitude to money.

Adults frequently use money to determine how 'deserving' we are as children. When we are "good" we deserve a treat or reward, but when we are not behaving as the adult would like, we are chastised with the withdrawal of pocket money or toys. Constant withdrawal can create a belief that we are generally undeserving or worthless.   'Worth-less' transmutes to become 'without worth', just as net-worth is sadly equated as self-worth. These are infectious behaviours indeed.

Phrases we hear like "money doesn't grow on trees" or, "money is the root of all evil" or, "we can't afford that" or, "never a borrower or a lender be" often contribute to the development of negative or false beliefs about money.

When you have completed your money story, ask yourself these questions.

•   How does your personal story affect your relationship with money now?

•   What beliefs, values or judgments about money are related to your personal experience and family history? Are they still active today?

•   Are they working to serve you, or not?

•   Are you having the kind of relationship you want to have with money or not? How could it be better?

As a Certified Money Coach(CMC)® and Couples Money Coach, I help people to identify and understand their money patterns, beliefs and behaviours using the system of Money Archetypes. This was devised by Deborah Price, the founder of The Money Coaching Institute. In her book, *Money Magic*, she introduces us to a set of eight characters, who help us understand the behaviours that exist inside all of us related to money. They are a powerful way of helping people to gain awareness about their relationship to money.

It is important to point out that the money types are not your personality type, or 'who you are'. Your money types can help you understand 'where you are' related to money.

A person may be showing the traits of several different archetypes, with each archetype showing up in different situations. By being more conscious of your habitual money behaviours you will be better prepared to change them when they occur.

Here are the descriptions of the eight money types.

The Innocent

This archetype takes the ostrich approach to money and doesn't want to see what's going on. The Innocent is easily overwhelmed by financial matters and seeks safety and security. They long to be rescued. They are the most trusting of all the money types. Like children, they have not learned to judge or discern other people's motives or behaviour. Whilst this innocent behaviour is fine for a child, it is precarious for an adult trying to cope in the big wide world. The Innocent often has a Warrior or Tyrant money type as a partner, as both Warrior and Tyrant thrive on rescuing the Innocent.

The Victim

Prone to living in the past and blaming their financial troubles on outside forces, Victims often live out a self-fulfilling prophecy. Sometimes they are disguised as Innocents as they seem powerless and appear to want others to care for them. Victims generally have a long list of excuses for why they are not more successful, blaming their past for their plight. Victims often have been abused or betrayed, but rarely have they processed their pain. Victims who are able to heal their past wounds, and release themselves from the attachment they have to their pasts make the most wonderful Magicians of all.

The Warrior

Goal oriented, focused, and decisive, Warriors tend to be the most successful as they are usually financially discerning, driven, and highly self-actuated. They can take charge and set out to conquer the money world. Warriors will listen to their advisers, but they will make their own choices. They rely on their own instincts and resources to guide them. The Warrior's biggest fear is losing independence and power. They may also need to recognise the difference between a worthy opponent and foe. A worthy challenger may incur conflict, but often has a great lesson to teach. The Warrior's task, financially speaking, is to ascertain what they really want to defend, and create boundaries around what is most important to them.

The Martyr

Martyrs are so busy taking care of others' needs they often neglect their own. They tend to be self-sacrificing and long-suffering. They may switch between being one who seeks to control others and acting as the needy child. Martyrs are financially generous but their generosity may have strings attached. Martyrs are perfectionists and have high expectations of others. They have the ability to reach their goals as they focus so much attention on being right. They see their glass as half empty and their focus on the negative often prevents them from seeing the great wisdom that they have through their life experiences.

The Fool

The Fool looks for a windfall and tends to take financial shortcuts. They are willing to take chances. The Fool is a combination of the Warrior and the Innocent. Like the Innocent they have difficulty in seeing the truth in things and have impaired judgement, but, unlike the Innocent, they remain optimistic whatever the situation. They are often impulsive and can get caught up in the enthusiasm of the moment. They are fearless and don't like to be defeated– like the Warrior. Unlike the Warrior, they lack discipline but they do have a tendency to fall on their feet! They need to slow down their financial decision-making process and do the research before 'signing on the dotted line'.

The Creator/Artist

The Creator Artist is often on a spiritual or artistic path. They find living in the material world difficult and usually have a conflicted love/hate relationship with money. They can be financially detached and have negative beliefs about materialism that block them from the freedom they crave. Being authentic is important to the Creator Artist. They are often loners. They possess many of the qualities necessary to become money Magicians and will become so, if they can accept the outside world and the realities of money.

The Tyrant

Tyrants use money to manipulate circumstances, people and events. They have a great need for safety and control and believe money is all that will provide that for them. There is a great feeling of 'never enoughness' even while they seem to have all they need. We see politicians, business leaders and family figureheads take the role of the Tyrant often seeking to win at all costs. Tyrants may be able to surround themselves with all they desire but may never actually be 'rich', as fulfilment is rarely found.

The Magician

This is the ideal money type. We are at our best when we are willing to claim our own power and become money Magicians. Armed with the knowledge of the past, Magicians are at peace with their personal history and money, feeling financially secure. The Magician knows their needs will always be met. Spiritual, wise, generous and financially balanced, they are awake and conscious of themselves and the world.

Which of the eight archetypes do you think are active in your life now? You may feel that one is taking the major role or that there are a few who run the show. The archetype that is active in your life right now is the starting point for your transformation. If you can understand the story behind your current money type, you will become aware of patterns and behaviours that are preventing you from reaching your goals – and becoming that Magician.

How do these beliefs, patterns and behaviours, these archetypes, show up in later life? Let me share Wendy and Alan's story with you.

Wendy's mother died when she was just six months old. Her father went on to have three further wives who took little or no interest in Wendy. Sent to boarding school at seven, with few visits home during holiday times, she was not really parented by anyone. Money was sent to school by her father. She never had to worry if there would be enough, or where it came from and when. Her belief was that she must be loved because there was always money for her. The fact that there were no parents to nurture and love her was normal for Wendy. The money continued to "arrive" during her college years and continued even after she met Alan. They married twelve years later.

Alan came from humble beginnings. His family had budgeted and managed their small income well, keeping their finances just about liquid. Alan had a notebook, where every expense was recorded. There was an Alan column and a Wendy column, it was tracked, analysed and balanced regularly. Everything was to be a fair split. Wendy was not used to this at all and tried to ignore it. Their disagreements were mainly over money.

When Wendy's father died, she inherited a large amount of money. Wendy thought that her new found wealth would last forever, but Alan thought differently. He urged her to be cautious and plan carefully for their future. With Wendy's belief that the money was endless, she hunted down big houses and new cars. Alan's opposing belief that the money should be managed with scrutiny, meant the rows grew and a rift was created between them. They divorced just two years after the money had arrived. By this time, they had two children.

Looking at the story so far, we can see both the Innocent and Fool archetype behaviour showing up in Wendy. The Innocent appears with Wendy's childlike behaviour upon receiving her inheritance. She was overwhelmed by the level of finance that she needed to understand. She had no concept of budgeting or investing. Her belief, formed from receiving the constant flow of money as a child, was that all would be well. No attention to detail was necessary.

Alan's persistence, and insistence that she deal with her wealth sensibly was seen as confrontation – and the Innocent does not like confrontation at all. Wendy put her head firmly in the sand and believed that her safety was her bottomless bank account. Her Fool archetype is there too. She wants big houses, new cars and lovely clothes. She spends freely without any clue of how much she is spending, and how the bank balance stands. Happy go lucky – all will be well. Financially irresponsible, optimistic and undisciplined – all the behaviour of the Fool archetype.

Alan had been taught great Magician/Warrior characteristics by his parents. He had learned how to look after his money carefully. He wanted to build assets and investments, whilst happily living a moderate lifestyle.

Looking at the reaction to Wendy's Innocent/Fool traits, it is possible to interpret Alan's expense notebook regime as Tyrant behaviour – being in control and controlling her. Whilst his intentions were good, her continued reckless spending habits pushed him towards critical and judgemental behaviour, sometimes with aggression. This will have only brought out Wendy's Innocent even more and may have even triggered her Victim. Victims also show financial irresponsibility. Whilst also feeling powerless, resentment can build, which is tricky to handle for the unforgiving Victim.

Wendy went on to have two further marriages and another child. Each of these marriages failed due to money issues. Eventually, her inheritance was spent. With a bank balance at near zero and very few assets to her name, the future looked bleak. Wendy was forced to take a long hard look at what had gone so horribly wrong.

I am not sure how Wendy found her Warrior/Magician but she did. She found strength and began to learn money management. She worked very hard collating her accounts together and created a plan to rescue the family from bankruptcy. Her two eldest children were at boarding school – just as she had been. The school was far away and home visits were rare for the children. As the money had run out, she had no option but to bring them home. However, she did see that a life far away, without close parenting, would probably encourage them to form the belief that she had – that it was normal not to have a parent close by, to provide nurture and that money fills the gap, by being on tap and that life is well. This was a pattern that she definitely did not want to encourage, so she looked forward to parenting them herself.

She did learn how her finances worked and set her goals high. She set up her own sandwich delivery service – which must have utilised a bit of positive 'fool' as she had no idea if it would succeed. She involved her children with counting the money, stock taking and working out profit margins on the sandwiches. A smart move and one that I was very happy to be a part of – as I was one of Wendy's children.

Alan continued to keep his book. In fact, he recorded every financial transaction he made to the end of his days. Having come from humble beginnings, with wisdom and goals, his anger at Wendy losing all that money was difficult to let go. He ended up with plenty of money but his Martyr played a major role in his life.

He was wise yet overly cautious with his money. Whereas he wanted to get the best return on the money, he would not consider the stock market or any risky investments. He relied on good interest rates while they existed, but made no change when they fell through the floor. He enjoyed giving his money away but there always seemed to be strings attached, which created discomfort for all involved. He lost friends through this. Many times, people failed to meet his expectations. The mark of the Martyr is an unconscious attachment to their own suffering. They switch between two very differing energies – one that wants to be in control and controlling of others and then the energy that feels like a wounded and needy child. This was very much Alan. I wonder what might have changed had he known to look at his money story and the Money Archetypes?

I believe understanding your relationship with your money is critical. I am so grateful and happy that I have had the opportunity to study my money story and work out which archetypes are showing up in my life. I have worked through issues that came up. This work is ongoing. Asking myself which archetype is in the room has become common practice for me and is so useful for keeping the negative archetypes at bay. As a result, I have been able to look forward financially and work out how I can reach financial freedom, which for me means being 'rich' by feeling fulfilled in every aspect of my life. For me, I have learned that it is not all about money.

But what about you? Where do you go from here? Are you aware where your Warrior and Magician are in the pecking order of the archetypes for you? Maybe it is time to get out pen and paper and look deep into your money story. Don't be afraid. Who knows what you might find? Who knows what you might create? The possibilities are endless and worthy of your exploration.

Fanny Snaith

About the author

Fanny Snaith – Financial Freedom Fighter® - Taking the Fear Out of Finance

Fanny Snaith lives in Cheltenham, in the UK. She is not an accountant or an IFA. In fact, she has never worked in financial services. She has, however, had plenty of experience with people and money. She has two children, a great husband and has worked hard on building a firm financial foundation to future proof them all.

Having watched her mother lose a large inheritance though careless spending and poor money management, Fanny made the vow to tread a different path. She trained and worked as a theatrical stage manager, worked in the television industry as a production manager and spent thirteen years as a credit controller for a consultancy firm with bases in the US and the UK.

Now working as a Certified Money Coach(CMC)®, Certified Business Archetype Coach, and Couples Money Coach she enjoys working with people to understand and change their relationship with money so that they can experience their greatest financial and personal potential.

Fanny is committed to helping the world better understand the meaning and purpose of money in our lives. She believes that talking about money, discovering and challenging our belief systems about money, can only make us and the world engage better with the wonderful tool and resource money is meant to be.

Visit Fanny's website to find out more about Money Coaching. Why not take the Money Type Quiz to find out what kind of relationship you are having with money now? All the info is found here: https://fffighter.com

Recommended reading:

Money Magic – Deborah Price

The Heart of Money – Deborah Price

Rich Dad Poor Dad – Robert Kiyosaki

Overcoming Underearning – Barbara Stanny

100 Tips for Saving Money and Getting Financially Fit

How is your financial health? Everyone can improve their financial health by considering a few of the following tips. The first step is always the hardest... it is just like starting a fitness program. Once you have started on the journey you feel great.

As with any change in health, small steps are simple, others take time or regular implementation to show the results across many areas of your financial life. But anyone can do them.

So what is the health of your hip pocket?

How To Shop Safely

1. **Write a list before you go shopping – and stick to it.** Food shopping forms a significant part of everyone's monthly outgoings and the supermarket is where the bulk of the money is spent. Never go to the shops without an idea of what you need. Don't put anything in the shopping trolley that's not on the list, no matter how tempting, and you'll come out of the store saving a bundle.

2. **Master the thirty day rule.** Whenever you're considering making an unnecessary purchase, maybe that new pair of shoes (of course they are not unnecessary), wait thirty days and then ask yourself if you still want that item. Quite often, you'll find that the urge to buy has passed and you have found another pair. By doing this you'll have saved yourself some money by simply waiting.

3. **Do specific shopping right after an event such as Christmas shopping after Christmas.** Get wrapping paper and cards after Christmas. The day after Mother's day get a Mother's Day card for next year. Get Easter egg decorating kits the day after Easter....no I am not saying buy the eggs and store for a year. You will find some amazing discounts and all you need to do is remember where you stored them!

4. **Don't go shopping when hungry**...you always seem to buy more when you do this.

5. **Do you need to buy designer labels**
    Celebrities are given expensive clothes to wear. You're not. At the end of the day, and let's face it you may only wear the outfit once, can you justify paying hundreds for a top designer that has had his or her name sewn on the label? These days, can you tell the difference? Think about it, maybe buy designer for a special occasion only.

6. **Learn to say 'no'**
    Well sometimes easier said than done....shopping with children..."can I have this?" say no or think about shopping by yourself. How often does a quick drink after work turn into more than you expected...wallet often a lot lighter at the end of the night. You don't need to say no all the time but a few times a year, can create some good savings

7. **Keep your credit card in a safe**
    That's right the safe....not your wallet – you will be amazed how much you save when you do not have access to easy cash or credit. Alternatively if you must use your credit card, ensure that you pay off the full balance each month.
    When you don't have access to credit it makes you think twice – do you really need it and if the answer is yes....it may mean a second trip to the shop giving you more time to think ....do I really need it?

8. **Buy staples in bulk.** Now if you are saying you don't have storage space, buy in bulk with a group of friends or neighbours. There are more and more stores offering discount bulk shopping opportunities and online as well.

9. **Take cash.** Taking only cash on a night out limits how much you can spend. Otherwise it's easy to get carried away and spend a lot more than we intended. Take advantage of happy hours!

10. **Always ask for a discount**. You might be amazed how often stores say 'yes'! We often do this when travelling overseas, so why not at home.

11. **Read your junk mail** – there are bargains to be had!

12. Check Unit Pricing at the Grocery store

Online Shopping Tips

13. **Remove your credit card numbers from your online accounts.** How easy is it these days to quickly buy online when most sites can store your card number….it is just a click and buy. The best way to break this habit is to simply delete your card from the account. That way, you will have to find your wallet in your big handbag….giving you time to think…"Do I really need this?"

14. **Sell your clutter on eBay**
I bet if you opened any cupboard or wardrobe you could find something you have not used in the last 12 months….interesting isn't it….so do you need it?
So why not sell them to someone else who does? Possibly on Ebay or have swap party with friends.

You can even save in your wardrobe

15. **Instead of throwing out some damaged clothing, repair it instead.** Don't toss out a shirt because of a broken button – sew a new one on. Simple sewing can be done by anyone – it just takes a few minutes and it saves a lot of money by keeping you from buying new clothes when you don't really need to.

16. **Go through your clothes – all of them.** Everyone loves to buy new clothes, so you are not seen in the same clothes each week…..so why not try taking the clothes at the back of your wardrobe and bring them to the front and suddenly your wardrobe will feel different. You'll feel like a brand new person….and your friends will think you have been shopping.

17. **Mix and Match your clothes** – you can dress minimally by buying clothes that mix and match well and this means you don't need as many clothes. With a few basics you can create a large number of combinations – also great idea for travelling to minimise luggage. Update your wardrobe with accessories rather than new items for a cost-effective fashion hit.

How can Family & Friends help you save money

18. **Give a gift of a service instead of an item.** Recently I gave a girlfriend an evening of babysitting so she and her husband could go out to dinner – she loved it and so did he. If you would love a pet but can't have one why not get a win-win and, offer to take care of friends pets when they travel...saves them dollars and you some pet time.

19. **Talk to your loved ones about what your dreams are, or ideas for gifts.** You may be asking "how does this save money?" Well, if they know what you like, they can buy items for you on that special occasion...or a few family members can get together and buy a larger item.

Can you save money with your banking?

20. **Always ask for fees to be waived or a discount.** Any time you sign up for a service of any kind and there are sign-up fees, ask for them to be waived. As mentioned before many times if you ask for a discount the shop assistant will say yes...all small discounts add up.

21. **Debt Consolidation** – if all else fails and you have overspent during the Christmas and New Year shopping period, consider refinancing credit card debt to a personal loan and contact Jan at Start Fresh Finance. Check what interest rates your credit cards and loans are.

22. **Change your attitude to your mortgage**
    The most expensive item you are ever likely to buy is your home. If you're not in the privileged position to pay cash, like most of us, make sure the loan you use to finance it is the best available. For example, if you are paying your lender's full standard variable rate, you are probably paying hundreds of dollars a year more than you need to.
    There are a large number of deals to choose from, so it is best to talk to a Broker who will do the research for you. Remember that loyalty to your bank benefits your bank, not you!
    Even better, if you can afford to make additional repayments on your mortgage, you'll clear your debt several years early and make massive savings.

23. **Clear your credit card debt**

    One of the golden rules of financial planning is to clear your most expensive debts first, in other words your credit cards.

    OK, credit cards can offer a convenient way to pay for goods and services but if you can't clear the balance every month, consider a low-cost loan as an alternative.

24. **Avoid ATM Fees**. Be aware of the ATM withdrawal fees charged by your bank. While some banks waive fees for all ATM transactions on any ATM machine, most don't. So be sure to use only those ATM machines where your bank will not charge the fees, or withdraw directly at your bank.

25. Save on your **electricity bill** by knowing what time is on and off peak. Using power at off peak is so much cheaper.

26. Review your **bank statements** every three months and see where you can save in the future and always check all transactions to make sure there are no additional debits.

27. **Draw up a budget**

    Can you achieve your goal without any additional savings? Or do you need to change your spending habits.

    If you are travelling as a family or couple, include everyone in the budget setting.

    Look at your current spending habits – where can you save – is it that third coffee each day? – you will be surprised that a small saving of say $3 a day can make a difference...could be $15-20 per week.

28. **Pay all your bills** when you get them; don't wait until they fall short of the due date. Sometimes paying early you receive a discount.

29. **Start a Piggy Bank**. If you drop your spare change in there you'll be surprised at how quickly it all adds up. It's a pretty simple, old-fashioned way to save and very effective (especially if you have a 'gold coins only' rule!!)

How to save on your Utility bills

30. **Cut the cost of your fuel bills**

    As the global demand for power threatens to outstrip supply, prices are rising. But that doesn't mean you need to be ripped off. Our utility market is a competitive one and you can change supplier with a few clicks of the mouse or by reviewing one of the many online comparisons.

31. **Consider installing a water tank**

    We often take our tap water for granted. And why not? But if it doesn't rain, and we are continually experiencing extended hot spells and drought periods, we should be looking for the best deal and ways to conserve water.

    Why not consider installing a water tank or water saving devices for your shower or even a timer on your taps for watering the garden.

32. **Cut your home phone bills**

    There are a large number of phone companies you can choose from and this can be very confusing, so again there are a number of businesses that specialise in finding the right solution for you.

    These days many people are re-considering whether they need a landline and mobile. Why pay for two phone numbers when you can only talk on one at a time.

    Good idea to regularly review bundles available that also include pay TV, mobile and internet.

33. Save **overseas calls** by signing up on Skype. It's free to sign up and calls are free plus you get the added bonus of seeing and hearing your loved ones.

34. **Consider a pay-as-you go mobile**

    If you do need a home phone and mobile why not consider as pay-as-you-go plan for your mobile. Review past mobile bills – do you receive value for money, do you really need all those minutes and texts that come as part of your package.

Insurance – A Must Have, so how can you save?

35. Don't automatically renew your insurances

Insurance is something that you cannot really cut out of your budget, but you should review annually. Can you afford to foot the bill if your house burns down? Or if you have an accident and cannot work, do you have sufficient savings for everyday expenses or even medical expenses. Probably not.

Again there are a number of online businesses that compare insurances for you or alternatively talk to an Insurance Broker.

36. You can ask insurance companies to **discount your premiums** if you take a multi-year policy; sometime you can save over 30 percent per year - you just have to ask!

Superannuation another Must Have

37. Life, total and permanent disability and income protection insurance can all be paid via your superannuation fund – easier on your hip pocket. **Talk to your financial Adviser**

38. Make sure you are not paying excessive fees. **Shop around** for your superannuation to ensure that you have a good balance of fees and return.

39. Take an **active interest in where the money is invested.** Consider how long you are going to continue to work and when can you access your funds – are they invested for the correct time frame.

40. Find your lost superannuation. Have you worked in a number of jobs since you started work? There are a number of internet sites you can find your super from past employment.

41. Consolidate your superannuation. Don't pay fees on multiple accounts!

42. Consider whether to **salary sacrifice.** This is something to discuss with your accountant or Financial Planner.

43. Depending on your income level, you could also consider the **co-contribution.** This is another item to discuss with your accountant or Financial Adviser.

There are savings when it comes to tax – and they are legal

44. **File your receipts** in a central location to maximise your tax deductions. If they are not filed together when you start your tax return you may forget some items.

45. **Pay all your tax deductible expenses before 30 June** each year and don't forget about tax deductions such as donations and income protection. Always get a receipt. If you are ever in doubt as to whether something might be claimable, get a receipt just in case!

46. Don't forget **work related deductions** such as self-education expenses, laptop/laptop bags, car and other travel expenses. You may need to keep a log book for your travel. Talk to your Accountant.

47. **Talk to a financial planner** or Accountant about your money and situation.

At work savings tips

48. **Split your weekly or fortnightly salary**
A great way to save, even if you don't have a planned trip on the horizon is to split your pay into different accounts – most employers allow you to split your pay saving you having to remember to transfer money.

49. **Carpool.** Is there anyone that lives near you who works at the same place (or near the same place) that you do? Why not ride together, alternating drivers each day? You can halve the wear and tear and fuel costs for your car.

50. **Find out about *all* of the benefits of your job.** Most people do not utilise all of the benefits available to them. Talk to your Human Resource department or search your company's website to find out about such benefits as salary sacrifice splitting of your salary, insurances, discount tickets, superannuation and often free financial advice.

51. **Take packed Lunch**. You can prepare the night before and put it in the freezer. By the time its lunch time, sandwiches will have thawed and be super fresh. It could save you about $60 a week! That's almost $250 a month!!! That's a lot of money!!!

How can Cooking Savings Tips save you money?

52. **Plan your meals around your store's special flyers.** Instead of just planning your meals based on a cookbook or whatever you can dream up, plan all your meals around what's on special. Look at the specials, then plan meals based on those ingredients and what you have on hand. Many of the stores also share recipes or suggested meal plans, you will find you will buy less and also use of items in your cupboard, thus savings on grocery bills.

53. **Eat breakfast.** Eating a healthy breakfast fills you up with energy for the day and also decreases your desire to have a morning snack.

Entertainment Savings Tips

54. **Don't pay full price for entertainment**
There are some amazing deals online now for a variety of entertainment – from activities for children at Theme Parks (well for adults as well) to theatre, dinners, weekends away and even overseas holidays.

55. **Walk/cycle to the station/work**
It's free and a great way to keep fit and healthy.

56. **An outing to your local library.** Don't look at a library as just a place to get old books. Look at it as a free place for a number of activities – books, CD's, DVD's, read the paper, internet and many other free events. The local library is a mecca for the money saver. You'll never need to buy another cookbook, guidebook or lifestyle manual again and if you can bear to wait a few weeks in the queue for the latest blockbuster, you never need to buy books again.

57. **Invite friends over instead of going out.** Almost every activity at home is less expensive than going out. Invite some friends over and have a cookout, watch a DV, play board games and have a few drinks. Everyone will have fun, the cost will be low, and the others will likely reciprocate not long afterwards.

58. **Swap babysitting with neighbours.** Does your neighbour also have children or a teenager that would like some extra pocket money? Taking it in turns for a night out to a couple dinner can make it a lot

more affordable and more regular thus saving money and working on a healthy relationship.

59. **Pack food before you go on a family road trip.** That way, instead of stopping in the middle of the trip, driving around looking for a place to eat, spending a bunch of time there, and then paying a hefty bill, you can just eat on the road or, better yet, stop at a park and stretch for a bit.

60. **Check out what your Council or local park has to offer.** My local area has regular free children movies in the park, play groups and even fitness or walking groups. A great way to save money with free activities and also stay health and fit and meet new people.

Where can you save Around the Home

61. **Turn off the television.** One big way to save money is to watch less television. There are a lot of financial benefits to this –less exposure to guilt-inducing ads, more time to focus on other things in life, less electrical use, and so on. It's great to unwind in the evening, maybe seek another hobby to do that.

62. **Be diligent about turning off lights before you leave.** So simple but how many times do you come home and find a light or fan left on.

63. **Buy appliances based on reliability, not what's cheapest at the store.** An hour's worth of research can easily save you hundreds of dollars. A reliable, energy efficient item may cost you more initially, but if it continually saves you energy and lasts for fifteen years, you'll save *significant* money in the long run.

64. **Start a garden.** Gardening is an inexpensive hobby and something you can do whether you have a backyard or even just a balcony. A great way to grow your favourite vegetable when they are in season.

65. **Celebrate Earth Hour** - it's not only is it good for the electricity bill, it is great for the planet... Try and have a mini Earth Hour in your household each month.

How to save while driving

66. **Keep your car tires at correct air pressure.** Just read your car's manual to see what the recommended tire pressure is, as this can improve your mileage. Tyres that are low on air pressure have greater rolling resistance. That means your car's engine works harder, using more fuel.

67. **Avoid Aggressive driving.** Aggressive driving habits such as excessive speed, abrupt braking and heavy-footed acceleration will lead to higher fuel consumption and more emissions. Reckless driving also increases the likelihood of your being involved in an accident, which may cause your future car insurance premium to increase.

68. **Use Cruise Control – when driving on open road.** For long drives on the highway or in country areas, try using the cruise control setting; it will improve your fuel efficiency.

69. **Remove excess weight from your motor vehicle** Increase your fuel economy by removing any excess weight from your motor vehicle – a common culprit is a boot full of heavy tools and equipment that are never used. Also remove any attachments such as heavy roof racks that are only needed occasionally; these can add significantly to the weight of your car as well as increasing wind resistance, further reducing your fuel economy.

70. **When buying a car, consider late model used.** These types of cars are often coming straight off of leases, meaning they were cared for by reliable owners. This is the same for business vehicles such as trucks.

71. **Don't speed.** Not only is it inefficient in terms of fuel usage, as it is highly cost-efficient to just drive the speed limit. Driving to the speed limit reduces your risk of an accident and fine by the police.

72. **Don't talk on your mobile phone while driving.** In addition to being very dangerous for you and others it is also incurs very expensive fines n loss of points on your licence.

Improve your health and in turn improve your finances

73. **Exercise more.** Go for a walk or a jog each evening, and practice stretching and some light muscle exercise at home. These exercises can be done at home for very little, meaning you've got an activity without a lot of cost, and the health benefits are enormous. Just set aside some time each day to get some exercise, and your body *and wallet* will thank you.
74. Next time you fill a prescription at the chemist, consider buying the **generic version**. They are chemically equivalent but usually cost less.
75. With **health insurance**, make sure you're not paying for things that you don't need. Private health insurance can be expensive but can save you a lot of money as well. Compare costs and features of funds – there are many businesses that do this for you.
76. Question whether you need the **vitamins** that you're taking – they can cost a lot of money!
77. **Prevention** is cheaper than a cure, so try to pay attention to your diet and exercise, to stay in good shape!
78. Get regular **health checks** from your doctor to make sure you're healthy. Check whether your health fund or your employer provides any benefits.
79. If you have a pet, investigate **pet insurance** for emergencies.

Children's Savings Tips

80. **Join your local playgroup** for a fun and inexpensive way to entertain the kids.
81. **Label your child's belongings**. A small outlay on nametags could save a large outlay on replacing lost items!
82. Be strategic about the number of **extra-curricular activities** they do. It's possible to have too much of a good thing! With regards to extra-curricular activities, try to organise cost-effective group sessions rather than one-on-one coaching.
83. If you are eligible, don't forget to claim any **government subsidies** or tax concessions/rebates.

84. **Teach your children** good spending habits by being a good role model.
85. Teach your children about the value of money by having them do **chores for their pocket money.**
86. Make it compulsory for **children to save some of their pocket money** on a regular basis. Some banks have excellent children's bonus saver accounts.
87. Buy kids clothes when the **big sales** are on, and buy the next size(s) up.
88. Call your **local community centre** and see what children activities they have to offer - you'll find they have a lot off free things to do!

Holiday Planning and savings tips

89. Have **travel insurance**. It won't save you money upfront, but could potentially save you heaps down the track!
90. **Sign up** for alerts for cheap airfares & cruises
91. When flying, see if you can manage with just **hand luggage**, or one suitcase between you to make the fare cheaper.
92. When possible, try to **travel off-peak.**
93. When booking accommodation, book a place with a **self-contained kitchen** to save a lot of food-related money.
94. Do **house swaps** as a fun alternative.....could even be international house swap. It's free! You can even swap cars with the other party.
95. If possible, try to schedule a **work-related conference** as part of your trip. This way your employer could pay for part of your travel expenses or they could be tax deductible. Check with your Accountant. Plan your vacation during **off peak season** and if you can, travel during non-school holidays to maximise on travel packages. Shop around and always be on the look out for promotions, sales and travel packages.
96. **When you go on holidays**, go around the house and switch off all the electrical equipment you don't need on while you're away, if possible empty the fridge out and turn it off.

Make More Money

97. As mentioned earlier sell unwanted good on EBay or a garage sale. **Spring clean** your home - One person's trash is another person's treasure!
98. **Be more assertive** in your performance reviews! Ask or a pay rise.
99. **Save, Save, Save**
Unless you are going to ask your boss for a pay increase you are going to have to work out how you can save money – cut something out of your regular spending routine.
You don't need to stop living and going out, often the small savings start to add up eg reducing the number of coffees, can actually save you a substantial amount each week. Or if you really need those coffees, how about a "Coffee Free Day"

Need Assistance - Ask for Help

100. **Never hesitate to get help**. If you are in financial strife or cannot see how you can reduce costs, take advantage of the free financial counselling service available.

Overall we all need to make a decision to cut costs. The right attitude is half the battle! Set a budget.

Select the tips that apply to you and use them in your life going forward– you'll quickly find yourself saving some serious cash and some of these tips can improve not only your financial health but also your health and well being.

As you incorporate more and more of these tips into your life, the savings add up and it wouldn't surprise me if you could save thousands over the course of a year…..and have that dream holiday.

Jan Watman

About the author

In 2013 Jan Watman took her finance experience and founded Start Fresh Finance. She leveraged her 20+ years finance experience to assist individuals and businesses to finance their dreams, whether a new car, boat or dream holiday or for a business a truck, earth moving or other business equipment to grow or expand their business.

Jan is a respected Australian business person, which was acknowledged as being one of the final 5 finalists in the Australian Telstra Business Women's Awards for QLD Corporate sector in 2011.

Jan's track record and experience makes her a sort after mentor and coach within the finance and sales environment. Her passion to help her clients shines through in all her dealings with them.

Start Fresh Finance is an Australian owned Finance Broking business that educates their clients on finance and sources the best loan for them to achieve their goals. Whether this be an individual or a business, Jan understands both, what the client needs and also what the finance company requires, thus making the loan process seamless, quick and simple.

Jan Watman – Director/Owner – Start Fresh Finance
0468371449
jan@startfreshfinance.com.au
www.startfreshfinance.com.au
http://www.linkedin.com/in/janwatman

How To Pay Off Your Mortgage 10 Years Sooner

It's true that mortgages are a long-term commitment, and it will no doubt be one of the biggest financial commitments you will ever make. But they don't have to last as long as you think.

Many borrowers fall into the trap of thinking they will be indebted to their lender for their entire loan term of 25 or 30 years. But I want to share with you how almost anyone can pay off their home loan 10 years sooner.

When it comes to mortgages, the proof is in the pudding. Australians need an increasing amount of money to retire and as such, they need to look at ways to optimise their savings potential as early as possible. By paying off your mortgage 10 years sooner you can save more money for your retirement and reduce the risk of having to return to work.

An analysis from one of Australia's biggest comparison websites finder.com.au of the Australian Bureau of Statistics (ABS) Retirement and Retirement Intentions report found a 12 percent increase in retirees intending to return to the labour force in 2013 because of financial needs. It's alarming to see so many retirees forced to go back to work because they can't afford to retire. No matter how much you earn, there are ways to help manage your money so you don't have to work forever.

Interest rate fluctuations can affect your ability to maintain a certain lifestyle if you retire with a mortgage. By paying your mortgage off early you can have peace of mind and the ability to plan your finances without the risk of interest rate changes. The Association of Superannuation Funds of Australia (ASFA) Retirement Standard report[10] shows that a couple looking to achieve a comfortable retirement needs to spend $57,195 per year, while those seeking a 'modest' retirement lifestyle need to spend $33,120 each year, but this number can increase if your mortgage repayments change.

---

[10] http://www.superannuation.asn.au/resources/retirement-standard

Living costs for retirees has increased and is likely to be causing the rise in retirees returning to the workforce. The ABS Pensioners and Beneficiaries Living Cost Index has grown by 2 percent in the September quarter 2013, compared with September quarter 2012. Some of the main contributors for the rising costs were housing with an increase of 5.2 percent, health which increased by 3.7 percent and a 3.5 percent rise in the cost of transport. These figures are in line with a report from Deloitte on The Dynamics of the Australian Superannuation System: The Next 20 Years, that show a 30-year-old worker on an average salary of $60,000 per year would have an estimated $1.1 million in superannuation at age 65 in 2048, but this amount would only sustain a comfortable retirement until age 77[11].

The number of retired men returning to work is rising, while fewer women are coming back to the labour force, according to retirees surveyed by the ABS. Our analysis revealed the proportion of males returning to work increased by 48 percent or 7,400 last year compared to the 5,000 from the previous year. Whereas women returning to work fell by 13 percent – 6,000 last year and 6,900 in 2012.

If you don't want to be a part of the 13,400 retirees who were forced to return to work in 2013, then you should explore all of your financial options to help improve your savings. By paying off your mortgage 10 years sooner you can safeguard your retirement funds and rest easy knowing that your money will see you through.

Outline of chapter
1. A little extra goes a long way
2. How to negotiate with your lender to get what you want

---

[11] Deloitte ' The dynamics of the Australian Superannuation System: The Next 20 Years' p28 http://www.deloitte.com/assets/Dcom-Australia/Local%20Assets/Documents/Industries/Financial%20services/Deloitte_Dynamics_of_Superannuation_2013_report.pdf

A little extra goes a long way

Mortgages can be complicated, and if you aren't confident in the features of your loan you may be missing out on opportunities to save. A home loan is something that will be with you for a long time, and making small financial sacrifices now can help you in a big way later on.

If you have a mortgage or are currently in the process of choosing a lender, you need to be aware of the possibilities offered by home loans to help you save money. By taking advantage of these features you can work towards paying off your mortgage 10 years sooner.

Additional repayments:
The first feature to look out for is the option of additional repayments. Lenders make their money from the interest incurred to you over the life of a loan, and so if you make additional repayments and pay off your loan sooner the lender will lose money. Because of this, some lenders charge a fee for additional repayments, or have a limit to how much you can pay per year, and some lenders do not allow them at all. This is often the case with fixed rate loans. Before deciding on a loan, you should check if you will be charged fees for additional repayments and if these repayments are allowed by the lender.

Lump sum repayments:
Lump sum repayments are also a feature you should consider when deciding on a lender. The payments involve depositing a large amount of money into your home loan early on to reduce the amount you owe. Lump sum payments added directly towards the principal of the loan, meaning the original level of debt is decreased, therefore reducing your interest charges. Lenders calculate interest on a daily basis, and so you can start saving on your interest almost immediately after making a lump sum payment.

Offset accounts:
Offset accounts are also a great option for borrowers looking to repay their loan sooner. An offset account is like a regular transaction account but directly linked to your mortgage account. The amount in the offset account actively reduces, or 'offsets' the principal loan amount. For example, if you

have a loan amount of $300,000 and have $10,000 available in your offset account, the interest is calculated on a balance of $290,000. You can use your offset account as a regular transaction account by making ATM and EFTPOS transactions or online via BPAY, all the while reducing the interest calculated on your loan.

Many offset accounts are 100 percent offset, which means all of the money in your offset account will be used against your home loan balance, so you only pay interest on the difference. Whereas some home loans offer partial offset, which means the money in your offset account only partially offsets your loan balance, usually with a reduced interest rate.

Another thing to be careful of is the cost as many charge ongoing fees of up to $15 per month, which may outweigh the benefits of the offset account.

Take a look at the case study below to find out what the possible savings are from using these features.

Case study 1: Jack and Alice
Jack and Alice are looking to increase their savings when they retire, and are considering options, which can help them pay off their home loan 10 years sooner. They have a $300,000 home loan at 7% p.a. interest over a 30-year loan term. Here are the options they have which can see them pay off their loan 10 years sooner.

Option 1: Additional repayments
Jack gets a raise at work and he and Alice review their budget. If they decide pay an additional $550 a month in repayments, they are able to pay off their loan 10 years sooner, and save $142,938 in interest which they can instead put towards their retirement.

Option 2: Lump sum payment
Alice receives a tax refund and decides to make a lump sum payment towards their mortgage. Using the tax refund and some savings, if she and Jack make a lump sum payment of $61,000 towards their loan, it will

allow them to pay off their mortgage 10 years sooner and save them $179,387 in interest.

Option 3: Offset account
Jack and Alice set up a joint offset account and if they can afford to keep $50,000 in the account by using their savings, they are able to pay off their loan just under 10 years sooner – nine years and three months – ultimately saving them $148,960 in interest charges.

Savings are calculated using home loan savings calculators available on finder.com.au, rounded to the nearest dollar

If you are already paying off a loan it is never too late to start accelerating your repayments. Whether you are five, 10, or 20 years into your loan term there is still a lot you can do to help you save money and pay off your loan sooner.

Case study 2: Morgan
Morgan is 10 years into a 30-year loan and has $300,000 left to pay. He wants to be able to have more money for his retirement and wants to pay off his loan sooner so he can save more money.

Using the historical average variable interest rate of 7% p.a., Morgan needs to pay an additional $1,000 a month to his mortgage repayments and will pay off his home loan a decade sooner.

By doing this, Morgan could also save $120,693 in interest, which he is able to put towards his retirement fund.

Savings are calculated using home loan savings calculators available on finder.com.au, rounded to the nearest dollar

To calculate the savings you can make from additional repayments, lump sum repayments or offset accounts you can use savings calculators online – there are a few handy ones on finder.com.au. You can input details of your loan such as your interest rate, loan term and amount, and then the amount of your extra repayments to your loan or offset to determine your savings, the new loan term amount and the amount of interest you will save.

No matter how far you are into your mortgage, depending on your loan amount and how much extra you can afford, you may be able to pay off your loan 10 years sooner.

How to negotiate with your lender to get what you want

It is common to feel overwhelmed by jargon and conditions set by home loan lenders, but it's incredibly important to stay in control of your loan. If you're new to the home loan market you need to arm yourself with information so you know what you're looking for and what questions to ask. You may have this loan for 30 years, so you want to be confident you've made the right choice.

You should learn about different lenders and the home loans they offer in order to have as much leverage as possible – be sure to compare the loans currently available on the market and understand how they work before you try to negotiate for a better loan. Existing borrowers should remain aware of market changes and better deals that are on offer so as to not miss out on any possible savings.

When comparing home loans, there are a few features that give you a good indication of the possible savings offered by the loan and the flexibility you will have when it comes to paying it off sooner. One of the main ways people compare home loans is by the advertised interest rate, which can be a good barometer of value, but this rate is not the main figure you should be looking at.

Lenders often advertise low home loan interest rates to entice borrowers to sign up with them. But these interest rates don't reflect the true cost of the loan. To determine this, you should look at the comparison rate, which is an effective rate and includes the interest rate for a loan amount and term, associated fees, averaged out over the loan term. You should also be aware that home loans can have tiered interest rates, depending on the amount of money you want to borrow or the loan to value ratio (LVR), which is the size of a loan compared to the value of a property (expressed as a percentage).

First home buyers

As a first home buyer you need to equip yourself with enough information to make the right choice. But another important part of the process is to be financially organised. Go through the application requirements on your lender's website and ensure you have the necessary documentation to apply. Home loan applications can be a lengthy process and they are often made longer because lenders have to chase the necessary documents from prospective borrowers. Necessary documents differ slightly between lenders, but generally you will need to provide:

- √ **Identification** - generally 100 points in total, this can include primary documents such as your passport or birth certificate (which usually make up 70 points), and secondary documents such as your driver's license (usually 40 points), or documents containing your name and address like land titles or council rates (35 points), or other documents with your name and address or signature like EFTPOS or Medicare cards, or lease/rental agreements (worth 25 points each)
- √ **Primary income details** - for this you will need to provide bank statements of at least the past three months, a letter from your employer, payslips or tax return statements.
- √ **Other income** - you will need statements detailing income earned from shares, managed investments, government income, superannuation or self-employed/income from a trust fund
- √ **Debts** - this includes personal loans and total credit card limits
- √ **Residential status** - you will need details of your real estate agent if you are currently renting.

✓ **Other documents** - you may also need details of your First Home Owner's Grant, details of other property purchased by you, details of building projects, monetary gifts, and/or your guarantor's details.

The thought of negotiating with a lender can seem terrifying, and this may lead you to think it is not worth it. But even as a first home buyer, you have a right to ask for a better deal, and if you're worried, just remember that the worst thing the lender can say is 'no'. Your home loan is a personal deal with the lender, and at the end of the day, the lender wants your business.

To successfully negotiate with your lender you need to have done your research so that you have a leg to stand on. You need to understand the kind of home loans the lender advertises and also the home loan you can afford. To determine that, you should draw up a budget and subtract your monthly expenses from your monthly income, and that should give you a good idea of the repayments you can reasonably afford. Once you have that number, you should also see what rates other lenders are offering so you can bring those numbers to the negotiating table. List the features or rates of a competitor's loan and ask why they don't offer the same, listen carefully to their answer, and then ask why you should not take your business to the competitor. They will be more flexible with costs if you are confident in your position and sound like know what you're talking about – even if you don't.

There are different components of a home loan which you should research and understand whether lenders are able to discount them. These include:
- **Interest rates:** These were historical non-negotiable, although during the past few years following the Global Financial Crisis, lenders have come to the party and matched a competitor's rate or may offer a discount.
- **Entry and exit costs:** Upfront fees is a common subject of negotiation, but exit fees are usually not. Some lenders will waive or reduce upfront fees, particularly if you are refinancing through the same lender.
- **Professional fees:** Some lenders will allow you to use your own solicitor or lawyer to take care of legal arrangements, granted they are appropriately qualified, and this can save you money.

Buying your first home can be a daunting process, but by informing yourself and being confident about your finances and your knowledge, you can work towards negotiating a better home loan.

Existing borrowers

If you already have a mortgage don't feel like you should just sit back and make your repayments for the next 30 years. You should keep yourself informed on market changes and of possibilities to save. It's important to perform a home loan health check regularly, ideally every one-two years, to make sure you're still getting the best deal for your needs.

You must ensure your home loan is competitive compared to the rest of the market, and to take into account your changing circumstances and how this might affect your home loan. The home loan you needed when you were 30 years-old may not be the one you need when you are 40 because you may need services and features which you didn't need a decade ago. For example, you don't need an offset account when you first have a mortgage because you most likely don't have any additional savings, but you may get a pay rise or another financial change which leads to an increase in your savings, meaning you could now benefit from an offset account.

In order to do a home loan health check, you simply need to review and compare your options. You should list all of your loan's features and services and ask yourself if you are making use of them, or if you even need them. You should also note the interest rate and fees you are paying. After that, review other options which are on the market and see if you could benefit from refinancing with a different lender. Financial comparison websites such as finder.com.au allow you to compare your home loan options and determine the best deal for you.

If you do find a better deal, you should consider negotiating with your current lender to match the loan. The growing number of lenders in recent years and the popularity of online comparison websites like finder.com.au, has resulted in increased competition in the home loan market, which is good news for borrowers. Armed with your research, all you have to do is call up your current lender and ask if they will match the interest rate or at least some of the features other lenders have on offer. When you call the lender you should be transferred to a loan retention department, whose entire job is to keep you from leaving, and can offer incentives for you to stay.

It's worth the call!

Twice within two years I personally called my home loan lender and asked how much it cost to switch lenders because I saw a better deal being advertised by a competitor. I asked if they could match the deal, and while they didn't match it, both times I received a discount on my interest rate. You should use the home loan market to your advantage, and by keeping informed you can save yourself money and even pay off your loan sooner. – Michelle Hutchison.

Whether you are a first home buyer or an existing borrower, do not be put off by lenders and the plethora of home loans available. Lenders exist in a competitive market and they want your loan. Do your research and compare home loans online to find a better deal to suit your needs. You may be surprised how easy it is to save 10 years off your home loan.

Michelle Hutchison

About the author

Michelle Hutchison is the resident Money Expert for one of Australia's biggest comparison websites finder.com.au, who loves to help consumers understand financial issues and how to find better deals that save you money. This is her first published book chapter.

Based in Sydney, Australia with her husband and two year-old son, Michelle heads up finder.com.au's PR team and is the company Spokesperson. She is recognised as one of Australia's leading Money Experts with regular media interviews and hundreds of published blogs and columns.

With more than five years' experience in the financial services and online comparison industries in Australia, Michelle is a big advocate of comparing financial products and has made it her mission to help more Australians find better.

After completing a Bachelor of Arts degree from Macquarie University in Sydney, Australia, majoring in media, Michelle began her career as a journalist in the newsrooms of radio stations 2GO and Sea FM as well as television news on Channel Nine's NBN News on the NSW Central Coast. She also worked in other media outlets including newspaper and magazine, climbing quickly to become Editor of Property Australia magazine before firing up her career in public relations.

Go First Class, Go Commercial

Everybody talks about a self-supporting life style but few will take the steps to make it a reality.

I have witnessed numerous people come to me to find out how I have been able to achieve that for my family. As an investor and developer for 35 years I guess I have the rungs on the board to be listened to. The interesting observation is that maybe 20% of those who come to me actually follow through.

That's a shame because my specialty is commercial property and through that medium I have been able to generate higher and more stable returns than in residential property. Most people stick with residential because it appears familiar and easier to understand. Really it's not, it's just people stick to what seems easier.

That preference means most investors are really not seeing he reality of better returns that are available with less risk if you structure your purchase correctly. So in this chapter I'm going to share with some gems learnt from 35 years in commercial property.

What's commercial property? It's the small street front shops, that little office your accountant occupies, that showroom, the tile shops, that small factory the mechanic uses. These are all owned by investors.

As a qualified Land Economist I love statistics as they provide a basis for decision making that isn't influenced by our own biases. The long-term return of commercial property is 13% per year and residential 12% what those statistics don't tell you though is the stability and management risks that are far lower with commercial.

Just type in Commercial property return UK or your own country into Google and the statistics are all there for you to read. As you will see and confirmed by many authorities on the economic clock we are about 7 to 8 o clock. This can be a good time to buy. It will also show you that over a long term commercial property provides very attractive returns.

So why commercial? What are the advantages? Let me list them for you. For ease I'm going to use Australian and UK rates, for other countries the numbers will vary.

1. The initial return is higher, almost double.

Investment return is made up of two things, rent and increase in the value of the property. The return is the amount of rent you receive divided by the purchase price. In residential the initial return ranges from 3% to 5% depending if its boom time or a recession. Commercial returns are generally 7% to 9.5% (UK 5% to 8%).

In the UK to Dec 2013 commercial returns had risen for 8 straight months. If you can borrow at 6% (UK around 3.5% to 5%) you already have a positive cash flow. Meaning your rent is higher than your mortgage payment even if you borrowed the whole amount. That has to be fantastic doesn't it?

2. You get a long lease.

When you rent out a home it's generally for a yearly lease then maybe the tenant will stay for another year. If not you will loose a month or twos rent whilst finding a new tenant. In commercial property the lease is for 3 or generally 5 years meaning you have the tenant for they long and don't have all those vacant months and leasing costs.

3. Every commercial lease has a fixed rent increase.

A home is leased for a year and then you may or may not put the rent up by $5 per month. In every commercial lease there is an increase built in every year of around 3% (through a consumer price increase, market rent or set percentage increase) that means over a 5-year lease you know the rent is going up by 15% at least. So if you bought a commercial property worth $500,000 then after 5 years you will have $75,000 increase in value virtually guaranteed.

4. The tenant pays all your costs.

Renting a Home can be a pain in the butt. Things always break down. New hot water system, toilet get blocked, the list goes on. You have to pay all the council and Municipal rates. In commercial property the tenants pays all these costs on top of giving you an 8% return compared to 4% for a house. So when you deduct the costs the return in the house is really about 2%. Guess which one is looking better?

5. You know more about the tenant that is paying your rent.

When you rent a house the amount you can find out about your new tenant is really limited. You can do a credit check maybe! You can talk to their last landlord if they rented before but really the information is limited. In commercial you can do a credit check on the company and it's Directors.

You can have the lease in the company name plus personal guarantees from the directors. You can have a check done on the directors and the property they own. In other words you get a lot of information to decide if these guys are a good or bad risk.

Let me show you the higher returns as well. Using the example above of a $500,000 property let's say you borrow against your existing house the $150,000 deposit you will need. If the return is 8% and you borrow at 6.5% then you have an excess cash flow of $7500 per year.

So over the first five years of ownership you get a set rent increase of 3% each year, which on the $40000 per year rent is $1200 in the first year.

Better returns

So in summary, assuming you already own a house and have equity; the money you already have sitting in your house (the difference between what you owe and can borrow) you will earn the following

Increase in value $75,000(based on fixed rent increases)
Increased rent from rent increase. $6000
Excess cash after mortgage payments. $37,500

Total return of your lazy $150,000 is $118,500.

No reason not to do it, is there?

What type of Property to buy?

Go for what you are comfortable understanding. If you don't know anything about factory units then don't buy one. If you would like to, do research on the market, talk to agents, get to know the critical factors for when you do buy. Office space is relatively easy to understand. A tenant needs some space to work out of and build a team they need space. That's where you come in as the landlord, so when you want to buy there are certain things you are looking for.

These are: -

Location
Don't buy out in the suburbs somewhere when you buy office space. Make sure there are plenty of other offices around where you buy and that demand for the area is high. That way if your tenant does leave at the end of a lease there will be likely be another seeking that space.

Buy early in the lease.
Most leases are 5 years so try to buy a property that has the location criteria satisfied then look for one that has a lease that is only in the first of second year. Then you can relax for the next few years knowing your tenant is going to be there.

Check out your tenant

Do the credit and other checks I mentioned to ensure your tenant is good for the rent. Again once you do you can relax. Talk to previous landlords, do a D&B credit history check, get three credit references from other companies they pay money to on a regular basis ensuring they do pay on time.

Get the right return

Most of your money is made in the initial purchase. If you buy at 10% return on the purchase price (cost $500,000, rent $50,000) compared to a 8% return, makes a 25% difference to your initial return, so focus on a great property at the best price available.

The second strategy is to buy a location that others don't want but makes good sense because of specific factors others haven't recognised.

As an example I purchased a property in the NW of Western Australia that was going through a mining expansion, there were only limited numbers of commercial property available and the building was fully tenanted. It was also available at a 13% return and the rents were very low in comparison to other similar properties and towns.

I held it for two and half years and received the rent increase and sold it at a 10% return at double what I paid. All because others hadn't correctly assessed the risk involved.

Find a property below the costs or rebuilding it

Commercial property is a great choice in comparison to buying residential. The best strategy though is to take the first step and begin to create an alternative income to working for someone else.

I negotiated the purchase of an industrial property for around $4m, which had a return of around 8% or $320,000 per year in rent. The land building would cost about $2.5m to replace making the land worth $1.5m. But when I looked around the area other developers were paying over $2m for similar land. Meaning the real value was about $4.5m for the property.

It also meant in a rising market that the developers would have to achieve much higher rents to justify building. So I knew the rents would have to go up. After just two years we sold the property for $6m just after a rent review.

There are many other methods of and techniques in finding a bargain in commercial property you just need to research it well, find a good mentor or advisor and always, always look for a bargain.

Don't be frightened it's only by taking a calculated risk will you get a great return. Take the first step.

Brett Jones

About the author

Brett Jones is a CEO of Entrepreneur Tribe an organisation dedicated to giving entrepreneurs the best lifestyle possible. Entrepreneur Tribe provides mentoring to investors to learn online how to invest in commercial property with trained mentors to guide investors through the process.

He holds a degree in Land Valuation from Curtin University and has owned or developed over $450m worth of real estate.

(The views expressed in this publication are the authors and are not investment advice. Before undertaking any investment, you should obtain the proper legal, financial advice from qualified professionals.)

Email ceo@cre8.com.au
www.cre8.com.au

Financial Freedom And Network Marketing

Network Marketing is a great business to be involved in; it gives people the opportunity to take control of their future both personally and financially. Anyone can get involved no matter what background or what age (as long as you are over 18) and that is the attraction. You don't need to be educated to the highest level and colour, creed, religion is irrelevant. As long as there is some energy, positivity and commitment, this business environment can work for anyone.

So what do you look for when you are investigating the opportunities out there? There are a number of key factors to look for. However, firstly draw yourself up a list of points that are important to you and make sure during your due diligence you have all your questions answered. There are some great companies who tick all the boxes, but beware of those that do not reveal the full picture.

It is important that you have a good feeling about your next step and that you feel relaxed and confident about the company you are about to join. There are too many people who leap, jump ship repeatedly and become serial networking catastrophes. This loses them credibility amongst friends and colleagues, makes them no money and also reflects badly on the companies involved.

The network marketing companies who are worth a look have a strong structure in place. There is no magic potion or "back door" quick way to make an income. Most companies provide a plan that works; it is all about joining, following the programme and staying with it for the long term , 3-5 years at least for starters and then the lifestyle kicks in so that work and way of life become one. The rewards will reveal themselves over time through financial freedom and enhancement in quality of life.

Here are a list of key points to look for when investigating a Network Marketing company

What are the Company Credentials?

OK, so how long has the company been operating for? Where did they start from and is the story consistent? Who started the company and is that person still heavily involved with the running of the organisation. Has the company always specialised in the same process or services or have they jumped around?

Is the company in profit, has the company grown in profits organically or by acquiring other companies? Look back through the financials; has there ever been a blip? If there has, don't automatically think that this is bad news; there may have been valid reason. Is the company transparent? Can you look back and investigate the history? Has there been steady growth or has the company grown quickly?

You are looking for Company longevity and organic growth

Is it Regulated?

Is the company a member of an industry body or regulated in anyway? There is the DSA www.dsa.org and other regulatory or bodies like Ofgem and Ofcom

www.ofgem.gov.uk

www.**ofcom**.org.uk

It is worth checking this out so that you feel confident that the company is operating within certain guidelines

Who is running the Company?

Who are the individuals? What is their business experience and expertise? Do they have people on the team who have knowledge of the products, services and, importantly, network marketing? Is there a relationship with leaders in the business and the management team? This is important to look for; you don't want to work for a company where there is no connection or communication with the distributors out there on the front line. There needs to be open, strong communication lines from inside out and vice versa.

What does it Cost?

People join network marketing for 3 reasons, to make money quickly, to build a business long term and to work on personal development. So how much is initial investment? Is it realistic? What are the chances of earning straight away? Can you get your money back easily? The whole point of this type of business is that individuals want to take control of their lives and finances. There is no point in joining if there isn't an opportunity to earn straight away. The recruiting and team building will take longer to generate significant incomes. Is there an instant pay scheme? That's important. The business needs to attract those who want a quick income fix and to attract those who want to build a long term income.

The other things to look out for are maintenance fees to stay on-board as a partner and whether you have to pay for marketing materials, brochures or extra stock?

Is There a Good Feeling?

I touched on this earlier. How does the company culture appear to you? This may sound a little too "touch feely" but for some people this is important. Do they have an ethos that reflects that they care? Is there a good, positive energy around the way the company operates? The meetings will often reflect this. Is there a connection between the Chairman or CEO and the network itself? Are they visible?

It's all about "The Money"

There are so many different types of compensation plans around. Look for **residual income** and if there is a cut-off point on the payment plan. Some plans will only pay down a certain amount of levels. Does the plan encourage partners to build their business deep through the different legs? Does the company insist on a certain target each month? A monthly target is not necessarily what people want, it puts pressure on and makes the whole thing look like another sales job. Residual income is the key here. You want to be paid regularly for doing the original work once. **You also what to check that the plan works in a way that you see success and reward if you help your team to do the same.**

Do you get paid for retailing the product? A strong business and down line will be built if payment is made this way. Payment on recruiting is good also; however this is a slower, longer term payment. If you and your team get paid on finding customers and you get paid an ongoing income (residual) for them to use the product, then this is a REAL winner. Look for this

What are the Products and Services?

Are the products single use or consumables? Does the company sell a product that everyone needs? Would you need it or use it? There are many products that come into vogue and then disappear just as quickly. There are gadgets and devices. Beware of being caught up in the excitement of a new piece of technology or equipment. These types of products pass through very quickly. Is the product or service something that is used every day? If there is stock, do you have to sell a certain amount each month? What happens if it doesn't sell, can you give it back? One of the common problems that some people experience in network marketing is that they have to buy certain about of stock each month and if not sold, it sits and gathers dust and cannot be returned. **So look for a consumable service or a product / service that people need. This is the key**

Looking into the Future

Is the company committed to moving forward with its technology and competitive edge? Is there a commitment to constantly research the market and also the ability to react quickly? How does the company match up to the competitors, not just in price but in quality, performance and aftercare? Are they ahead of the game, always watching and even better, one step ahead? What are the strategic plans for the company's long term presence and success?

The Customer is Right

Customer Service is an important way of reflecting how a company looks out there in the marketplace. A good reputation is a critical if the company is to distinguish itself from competitors. This will help you enormously. It will give you confidence and belief that you have the support of a great team back at HQ. It's all very well offering a cheaper service but is the quality still good and does the customer get great support after their purchase. Would the customer come back to buy other services from the company. Can they add on? What is the level of service here? Does the company commit itself to ensuring that the aftercare and support top the customer is at least 100%.

The best way of testing this is to become a customer yourself. Not only will it give you very good idea of how the systems work but will also give you credibility when talking to others about the company or service. If you are not a user, how can you deliver an authentic message to your prospective customers?

Your Training, Development and Support

The training programme in a Network Marketing company is vital to the life blood of the distributors. The important part to look for in a training programme is ease of use, accessibility and cost. Network Marketing businesses are built on finding customers and finding recruits. If the new recruits don't know what to do and can't access comprehensive support and training easily then they are going to do nothing. The system must be "PLUG & PLAY" so that everyone can access the trainings easily and be able to duplicate the message down to their teams. These days an online training programme is essential with an in-house training in addition so that the distributors can connect with leaders and other colleagues

Check that there is sufficient training detail on the products or services you are going to be talking about. The training programme must be accessible. No one is going to learn everything in one session. So check that the training can be revisited over and over and for free. Knowledge brings confidence and belief.

Also check how the company is moving forward in developing the training. When changes are made or new products are introduced, is the training refreshed at the same time? What does the company invest in training and is there a dedicated team who work on this resource?

Is there an ongoing development programme in place?

Building a networking business is not just about the products and services. As individuals pass through time they will have different needs and requirements. Most network businesses are built towards a certain structure. As the experience and business builds, as well as the income, then different skills are required to consolidate and develop individuals into leaders in their own right. What is the ongoing personal development and training programme like? Is there something for someone who wants to learn leadership skills or recruiting skills, advanced leadership skills or goal setting skills?

Training programmes need large quantities of investment so how is the company doing in this area?

Working Tools

The whole point of the marketing is that the partner or distributor carries the brand and services out to the consumer. What route to market do you have and what can you use? Brochures, posters, meetings, word of mouth, internet, social media, and events. Are there any other messages or platforms that the company delivers which help the partners themselves? Does the company help you by contacting customers directly in a positive way? Will there be a website that you can use and what are the costs? How will you be compensated if there is a dedicated website for you to market the product through? Are there any rules and regulations on how you get the message out?

Does the company insist you run special meetings or is there a Party Plan method in place? In Party Plan, customers are found during meetings held in homes mainly in the evening .The whole point about network marketing is that the business can work flexibly around family and lifestyle. Being out every evening running events can be draining in time and energy and family relationships.

Building the Team

This is another aspect of the business that needs marketing. Sure, you can do this by talking to people but what extra provisions are made for you to get a message out about the business opportunity? You are looking for many options here so the more the better. Each person who investigates the business opportunity will have different needs in how they gather information. It is a fact that individuals looking at business opportunities will need more than one piece of information. So are there DVD's, booklets, information packs, brochures, online videos, scripts and presentations available for you to use if and when you need.

Does the company organise and run regular presentations at easily accessible location so that anyone can go along for a look? Are these meetings free or is there a charge? Who runs the meetings, how long are they? You are looking for short, professional, punchy, and "non hype "meetings. It's best that they are run by successful leaders who can readily support and answer queries at the end.

Summary

So if you want to change direction, get off the treadmill, build a business that fits around your life, or work on your personal development then this is a business for you. Network Marketing is the environment for people who love working with people and want to have fun. Just remember that you will have to put the work in for a while, but not forever like a normal job!

Ruth Warlow

About the author

Ruth Warlow trained as a State Registered Nurse in the Radcliffe Infirmary in Oxford in the mid-seventies. After moving for work to South Africa she was offered a sales position in the healthcare sector.

She visited hospitals all over the country with a range of new products to increase the quality of patient care. This took her to Soweto, Ga-Rankuwa and Baragwaneth hospitals as well other provincial hospitals and the private sector.

Ruth returned to the UK where she worked in Healthcare Sales Management for a number of years. In the 1990s, wanting to get out of the Rat Race and a punishing schedule, she left the healthcare industry and ran a number of small home businesses promoting natural plant and eco-friendly products. Ruth also trained as a fitness therapist and held classes in Body Conditioning and later, Yoga Therapy. She ran Mind Body Yoga in the Thames Valley for 10 years.

Ruth worked a few hours a week for a business colleague and friend in telemarketing, sales and PR and it was at this time she set up her Network Marketing Business with The Utility Warehouse Discount Club. She worked her business alongside for six years and then committed to full time.

Ruth is now a Group Leader, Trainer and Mentor, has a group team of 1000 distributors and is in the Top 1.5% of the Leaders in the company. She drives one of the company's branded BMW Minis and has won 2 international holidays, share options and other company awards. She has spoken and trained at company events and works closely with her growing team.

Ruth is based in the Thames Valley with her son Tom and lives life to the full. She enjoys keeping healthy, walking, skiing, photography and the outdoors. Her personal message is; "Just do it and do it now!"

www.RuthWarlow.com

www.take150seconds.co.uk

https://www.facebook.com/pages/Simply-Wealthy/15059458841400

LinkedIn: Ruth Warlow

Twitter : RuthWarlowUW

Network Marketing and Financial Freedom In Two To Four Years

Financial freedom is something we all strive for, yet in this day and age very few ever achieve. Earning a big salary is often seen as financial freedom, but often it is not the case! How do you gauge your financial freedom? I believe the best indication is to ask yourself, "If I were to stop working today, how long could I survive while maintaining my current lifestyle?"For people with high salaries this may only mean six months, a year, or even a couple of years for the extremely high earners. For ninety-five percent of people the answer is a couple of weeks or even just a couple of days.

True financial freedom is to be able to stop working all together and still maintain the lifestyle you are living now. In network marketing, if you build your business correctly, not only should it keep paying you the same amount when you stop working, but it should keep growing without you.

Traditionally, the key to financial freedom lies in your ability to build systems that duplicate and run without you. McDonalds is the ultimate example of this with over 29,000 duplicated systems (stores) and an annual revenue of over $40 billion. The other way to make money without being required to work physically is investing, however it is not without it's pitfalls. The problem with investing in property for example, is it is much slower than it used to be. We have to wait for the properties to be paid off and accumulated before we actually bring in a healthy cash flow, which can take years and involves a large amount of capital.

Network marketing, an industry that has been somewhat misunderstood, has survived the pyramid allegations and the chain letter and ponzi scheme days. The industry is now emerging not only as a viable option, but some suggest it is the best way to create financial freedom in two to four years. Network marketing is now being endorsed by some of the most well known and successful business and wealth advisors. These include Robert Kyosaki (best-selling author of Rich Dad Poor Dad), Harv Eker (author of Secrets of the Millionaire Mind) and the famous Billionaire, Donald Trump. Network marketing can now be seen in publications such as Forbes, Fortune and Success magazine and even "The Oracle", Warren Buffett, is now investing in several network marketing companies.

The network marketing industry currently does well over $120 billion per year and economists such as nine-time best selling author and two-time US Presidential advisor, Paul Zane Pilzer, suggest the real growth has barely begun. Pilzer, among other top forecasters and advisors, believes we are heading into the golden era of network marketing and up to 40 million people will join the profession in the next few years alone.

Why are so many people predicted to head to network marketing and why are so many people endorsing it? The industry has cleaned itself up and has heavy code of ethics, with bodies such as the DSA (Direct Selling Association) ensuring their partner companies have sound operating practices.

The growing number of millionaires being created through the network marketing industry is certainly boosting its attractiveness, but the real reason I feel is that more and more people are waking up to the fact that their jobs aren't going to provide for their retirement and a decent lifestyle. People today simply can't afford to try other methods like franchising or starting their own company.

Network marketing gives every day people the advantages of buying a franchise, without the overheads, risk and the ability to expand it to an unlimited level. Network marketing is also becoming a popular addition to peoples folios. A residual income of just $300 per week can be considered the equivalent of owning a $300,000+ apartment.

My experience with network marketing began in 2011. I had been through 13 different careers, tried to launch several business and had accumulated a massive debt. I didn't aspire to be a professional network marketer growing up and I fell into it, as I really had no other options. I knew I was never going to get rich working a job for somebody else, I didn't have a cent to my name and the banks wouldn't touch me. It turned out all of these failures were a blessing, as it lead me into an industry that not only earned me a great income, but taught me skills from presenting, sales, leadership, managing and dealing with people, to working with and developing systems, running events and working on my self-development.

Traditionally network marketing has been dominated by professionals well into their thirties and older, however I was able to build a team of Gen Y entrepreneurs, who were hungry, knew very early on that the traditional nine to five work system was broken, and were looking to build success fast!

Having a great residual income through network marketing opens up other avenues: you are not locked into office hours so you can allocate time to look at property to invest in, to view shares and stocks or pursue any other ventures you choose. Having residual income means you can take more risks. If something falls through you still have a strong income of five,ten, twenty or for some people fifty thousand dollars per week coming through.

As the economy crashes most industries are negatively effected, however the network marketing industry is one of very few that thrives. As people become more concerned about their pension, their retirement funds, inflation and lack of job security, they are forced to look outside the box and look at options in the home-based business field. They will do anything to create another stream of "now" money.

So how does network marketing work? Well, I like to compare it to the franchise model that all of us already understand. In any franchise such as McDonalds, Starbucks or Anytime Fitness, they all started with one location. The first goal was to bring in customers and create repeat business. This is exactly how you start your network marketing business: you get started, learn the skills and bring in a customer base.

For the franchises mentioned above, if you want to get to more customers, you need to expand to more locations. More locations means more customers and more customers equals more money.

This is how the real wealth is also created in your network marketing company, however it requires far less financial investment. You are not required to find other franchisees who need to invest hundreds of thousands of dollars for you to reach more customers. In network marketing you build a team of independent sales reps, who can usually get started for less than a thousand dollars, while buying products they can use.

The advantages of network marketing versus franchising is the reps have the same opportunity to expand as the owner does. In the Mcdonald's system, only Ray Croc was able to expand and leverage off thousands of stores. The franchise owner, although spending millions in some cases, will need to spend another million to open a second location.

An obvious advantage of network marketing is there is no large capital risk involved. However, this can backfire, as when someone only spends five hundred dollars on a business, they often don't take it seriously. This is despite the fact this vehicle can earn them far more than any franchise.

The best parts of a network marketing business are that you can go at your own pace, you can't fail and if you fail for twelve months you don't lose a cent. As a network marketer, you will have a mentor who has a vested interest in your success helping you every step of the way. Its truly an incredible business model that I believe everyone should try at least once!

If you are looking to get involved with network marketing, you can take advantage of another booming trend, which is the health product industry. Currently doing around $600 billion annually it's predicted to reach a trillion dollar industry in the next five years alone. In life, the greatest problems create the greatest opportunities and there are no two bigger problems than health and finances in today's world. This makes a health networking marketing opportunity the ultimate vehicle heading into the years ahead.

The future for network marketing is enormous with just about every finance book, magazine, speaker on wealth and the media endorsing the industry. There are now endorsements from numerous celebrities and high profile sporting teams, which are strengthening the entire industry.

The nine to five work day model is broken and people are starting to realise they can't live the life they want working a job. Retail is dead, franchising is hurting and the property market is slow, leaving one of the greatest entrepreneurial opportunities in history, network marketing, for those who are open enough to investigate it a little further.

Things to look for in a network marketing company

-DSA approval (the governing body ensuring the company is legitimate).

-You have a consumable product- no one wants to work on one off sales.

-You have a universal product that a large majority of people will use.

-You have a product people need.

-The company is three years old (over 95% fail in the first 18 months).

-Ensure they have clear training and a duplicatable system (the best product won't sell without a great system).

-You like the people involved (at the end of the day people don't buy products, we buy people).

-The company is well run (back office, customer support etc).

11 Tips for Success in Network Marketing

1. The law of process

Most people quit far too early and miss the big results the law of process pays out. Some of my best reps signed up 12 – 24 months after first pitching to them. This industry (and any) pays to the people who stick out the journey. Remember this a 2-4 year plan, not 2-4 month one.

2. Make sacrifices

No successful person on the planet has got where they are without making time and financial sacrifices, yet nearly no one is willing to sacrifice either. Make the time and financial sacrifices today to get the time and financial freedom tomorrow.

3. Manage Your Emotions

Warren Buffet said it best, saying "If you can't manage your emotions, you will never manage money". You need to control your emotions and not have them controlled by the action (or inaction) of others. Toughen up, this industry like any business will test you!

4. Share a Big Vision

Not having a vision and having a big vision you can't share are the same thing. No one will rally and work this business hard enough to become successful without a big vision. So share big and create a team filled with passion and excitement.

5. The Little Things Make the Big Difference

The one percent-ers and finer details may seem small and petty, but the fortune lies in it. Your attention to elements like the music at an event, the extra courtesy call or follow up MATTERS!

6. Passionately Serve Others

If your team or customers success aren't your highest priority, they will go to a business where it is! Look after your team and they in turn look after you!

7. Simplify Everything!

If you can't simplify it, you don't know it, and your prospects certainly won't get it either. Talk in concepts and recap all detail, referring back to simplicity.

8. Be Likeable

Sounds easy, yet possibly the hardest to master. People not only buy off people they like, they buy off those they are like. Pretty simple, relate to all and don't be a "douche".

9. Prepare Everything

Your preparation for meetings, trainings, presentations, objections, your day, your week, your year all matter! Prepare each day like Roger Federer would a grand slam final.

10. Ignore the Naysayers

Be more upset if you don't have critics, as all successful people have them as a bi-product of their success! It takes no talent, skill or courage to be a critic, so don't waste your emotional or mental energy with these people and keep your eye on the prize!

11. Lead By Example

Far too many people jump into micro-management mode too quickly. The most respected general is one leading in the field, so have integrity and do what you preach.

12. Loosen Up & Smile

People get so serious and tense when talking business. Chill out, have fun and enjoy the process. Being too tense or over serious screams amateur. Smiles and a relaxed, composed nature projects success.

Dave Nelson

About the author

Dave Nelson is a network marketing professional. He is one of the top earners for American founded health company, YOR Health.

Dave started his business in Australia at just 23 years old.

Now 26, he enjoys financial freedom and an affluent lifestyle, which many can only dream of.

Dave is classic network marketing rags to riches story, Today he is still in the field, continuing to build business, while passionately promoting the network marketing industry as a whole.

Taxing Times

Developing tax efficient investment strategies

I've spent over 20 years in the wealth management industry and in my experience the area which is most neglected in the majority of cases is taxation.

I have never met a client who would choose to pay more tax on their portfolio than is absolutely necessary. However, I cannot remember the last time I had a meeting with a potential client whose tax position could not be dramatically improved.

Tax planning in relation to investment portfolios seems to fall through the 'advice gap' between the investment adviser, who is focused on the returns and risk of the portfolio, and the accountant who assumes that the adviser is taking care of it.

I have often come across tax planning solutions which may have looked attractive initially but actually result in more tax being paid in the long term. I have also seen numerous cases where the tax planning was correct when the portfolio was established but, because there was no on-going active tax management, the position slowly deteriorated over time.

Part of the problem is that it is easy to focus on the negative aspects of tax because it feels as if we get taxed at every turn. When we earn money, we pay Income Tax and National Insurance (these are actually the same thing but for PR reasons, it suits the Government to have separate names and base them on slightly different calculation methods). When we have spent what we need to live on, we then save the balance. If these savings generate an income, then we pay more Income Tax. If we make a gain, we might have to pay Capital Gains tax. Finally, what we haven't spent by the time we die might be subject to inheritance tax at 40%. Even tax efficient vehicles such as pensions can have hidden traps in that if you die at the wrong time with money in your pension, or you simply accumulate 'too much', you may get hit with a whopping 55% tax penalty.

The rates of tax can also be baffling as the current rates of tax which could apply to a typical investment portfolio are 10%, 18%, 20%, 28%, 40%, 45% and 55%. So, with at least four different taxes and seven different rates, the matter can prove to be overwhelming and disheartening.

However, I believe the current regime in the UK is actually very accommodating towards savers and, if you structure your savings correctly, the vast majority of investors should pay almost no tax at all. Even a wealthy individual with a portfolio worth many millions should be able to legitimately reduce their tax to an overall rate in the region of 10% - and still enjoy a six figure income.

So let's get started and look at some of the ways to mitigate tax on your savings and investments.

Step one - ISAs

These are the foundation stones of a tax efficient portfolio and the best place to start. They are one of the few investment areas where the taxman is helping you save for the future.

The first ISA rule is to use your full allowance every year because if you don't use it you lose it. Every individual can contribute up to £11,520 (in the current tax year) per annum and not have to pay either income or capital gains tax on the returns.

Start saving as soon as you can and pay in as much as you can – the benefits over time can be staggering. I have many couples as clients who have got ISA portfolios of more than £1million which gives them a tax free income and access to capital.

Next, think about how you fund your ISAs. One clever strategy is to sell any directly held, taxable investments, once a year to fund ISAs. This uses up your annual Capital Gains Tax allowance; everyone can crystallise gains of up to £10,600 per annum at the time of writing with no capital gains tax payable. If you use this each year it prevents a big capital gains tax liability building up over time, avoiding tax at 18% or 28%.

I would always recommend investing in a 'stocks and shares' ISA as, logically, a potentially higher return therefore maximises the tax efficiency.

Step two – the right type of return

When you are investing, you need to understand how the different elements of the returns you achieve will be taxed. Let's say you place your money in the bank and they pay you interest, this interest is all subject to income tax unless it falls within your allowance (see below).

If however, you invest in an investment 'fund' such as a Unit Trust, then the tax is slightly more complicated. The "return" you enjoy is actually likely to be a combination of income and capital growth. The income elements may be subject to income tax and the capital element to capital gains tax.

That may sound logical but it is unfortunately not that simple as there may be dividend income to take into account which is taxed differently again. Through careful fund selection you can pick the right fund with the right mix of returns to minimise your overall tax liabilities.

Step three – use your allowances

Make sure you make the most of those tax breaks that the Government has kindly given and don't waste the opportunity to mitigate the amount of tax you pay.

1. Income Tax

Dependent upon your age, every individual is given an annual allowance of £9,440 (current tax year) before they have to pay any income tax. It is often possible through careful structuring of a portfolio to limit what is classed as 'income' to this level so no tax is payable.

2. Capital Gains Tax

Firstly, each individual is given an annual exempt amount of £10,900 before they need to pay tax on gains. This is a very generous and under-utilised allowance.

Secondly, the tax is ONLY payable when you "cystallise" a gain. In effect, this means you can roll up gains for many years, not only deferring payment of the tax but achieving growth on the tax that you would have paid otherwise.

Thirdly, the rates are lower for capital gains tax than they are for income tax at 18% versus 20% for a basic rate taxpayer and 28% versus 40% for a higher rate taxpayer.

Finally, if you allow the gains to roll up until death, then the tax liability dies with you and there is no capital gains tax to pay! Although I'm not suggesting that this approach should be taken in isolation as there are other ways to mitigate the tax during one's lifetime too.

Let's look at a simple case study which might help demonstrate how these two tax allowances can be used in conjunction to create tax efficient returns.

Harry is 65, has just retired and enjoys –

- A state pension of £7,000 per annum
- An ISA portfolio he has built up of £250,000 from which he withdraws 4% per annum, i.e. £10,000 tax free
- £100,000 in a building society which pays him 3% per annum (£3,000) which is subject to income tax

- £150,000 in a unit trust which is subject to income tax on income and capital gains tax on gains.

Within the unit trust, he invested in UK Equity income funds and the yield on the portfolio is 2.50% which provides him with £3,750. As it has been a fairly good year, the capital has increased too, by 7% and providing a gain of £10,500 which he withdraws to supplement his income.

So, let's look at the overall position.

- TAXABLE INCOME – the State Pension and his deposit interest total £10,000. His personal allowance is £10,500 so the income tax to pay is zero.

- TAXABLE GAINS £10,500 – the gain from his unit trust falls within the annual capital gains tax allowance so the tax to pay is zero.

- DIVIDEND INCOME £3,750 – no personal income tax (although notional 10% tax credit applied)

The total amount Harry has enjoyed has been a healthy £34,250 in the year - and he has not paid a penny in income tax. In fact, the story gets better as Harry is married to Sarah who has structured her portfolio in exactly the same way so combined they enjoy almost £70,000 of income and pay no tax.

The key to making the most of our favourable tax regime is structuring your investments correctly so that you can utilise the available allowances. You can also consider investing money in the names of other family members to utilise their allowances too as even a baby has their own income and capital gains tax allowance.

Step four – get a pension (and get one for the kids too)

Despite the bad press and the Government's constant tinkering with policy, pensions remain one of the most tax efficient strategies. The benefits can be taken advantage of by anyone from birth to age 75 and, once held within a pension, income and gains are tax free, just as they are in ISAs.

Virtually everyone can put at least £3,600 a year into a pension, even if they are not earning. You just need to invest £2,880 and the Government will gross this up to £3,600 – a 20% boost overnight. The compounding effect of growth on this tax relief makes a huge difference over the long term.

There is tax relief at your highest marginal rate on your contributions, there is tax efficient growth within the fund and then you are able to get 25% of the value out as a tax free lump sum from age 55.

Build up your fund to a size where the value, after taking your lump sum, can provide an income within the basic rate tax band. Alternatively, consider a drawdown strategy where you can vary the amount you take out on an annual basis to take account of any other taxable income you may receive.

For the family, it's worth noting babies born in 2014 will be 77 years old before they receive a state pension.

A combination of high student debt, rising house prices, low annuity rates, withdrawal of final salary pensions and living longer in retirement has created a 'perfect storm' meaning that creating a pension pot big enough to stop working at a traditional retirement age will be out of reach for many of the next generation.

If you invest the maximum contribution of £2,880 net/ £3,600 gross over four years for your child from their birth, this could be worth £2,658,761 at an age of 65 if you achieve 9% annum growth.

Even just one contribution can make a significant difference creating almost £10,000 of income in today's terms, by the time the recipient reaches the age of 65.

This strategy has proved so popular that to date, 20 per cent of our clients have set up over 180 pension policies for their children or grandchildren.

Step five – investment bonds

Another vehicle to think about is an investment bond. Historically, this type of product has taken a bit of a battering from having been mis-sold and mis-used. However, used in the right way, they can be very tax efficient.

Let's assume that our aforementioned friends, Harry and Sarah, won £1million via a lottery scratch card. Having already invested some of their portfolio for the benefit of their six grand-children, they don't yet feel in a position to give away their windfall. An investment bond could prove to be ideal in their circumstances as they already regularly use their capital gains allowances. For instance –

- Indexation – gains within a bond are first offset against retail price index (RPI) before any tax is due. So, if RPI is 3% and the gain is 3%, there is no tax to pay. On £1million, that's the equivalent of a £30,000 capital gains allowance!
- Dividends – dividends received within the fund are not subject to further tax
- Internal taxation – gains above RPI and any income received other than dividends is taxed within the fund
- Personal taxation – 5% of your investment can be withdrawn annually with no tax to pay until you decide to fully or partially encash the bond
- Top slicing – a calculation to determine whether there is any personal tax to pay when the bond is surrendered. Take the gain, divide by the number of years invested and add that amount to your taxable income. If you remain within the basic rate tax band i.e. £41,450, there's no further tax to pay.

Step six - time to be generous

There are several methods of reducing the value of your estate in order to mitigate a potential inheritance tax charge. Firstly, take advantage of annual exemption which means you can currently give financial gifts up to the value of £3,000 per annum which is free of inheritance tax. This is a great opportunity to help your loved ones start saving for the future and reduce inheritance tax bills at the same time. If you miss a year, you can carry forward the exemption to the following year.

Also, don't forget about the small gifts exemption where you can make gifts up to the value of £250 to as many people as you like in any one tax year.

If you want to make regular gifts, these can also be exempt from inheritance tax if you have enough income left to maintain your normal lifestyle. There's no maximum amount with this exemption either, so you can give away as much as you like providing it's a 'regular' payment and doesn't have an adverse effect on your standard of living.

Charitable gifts are exempt from inheritance tax too and if you want to give charitable donations make sure you use Gift Aid. Gift Aid increases the value of donations to charities and community amateur sports clubs (CASCs) by allowing them to reclaim basic rate tax on your gift. If you pay higher rate tax you can claim extra tax relief on your donations. For more information on how to give using Gift Aid look on the HMRC website.

I believe that inheritance tax is a voluntary tax but I also understand that individuals need to be confident about their own financial future before they feel able to give money away. Create a plan, have a strategy and build that confidence!

What next

Wealthy investors should be asking their investment advisers how they plan to mitigate the tax before they even begin to discuss how they are going to achieve the returns. Creating a tax mitigation strategy does not involve using complex schemes which will attract the attention of HMRC or that may come back to haunt you. It simply involves taking a holistic view of your overall affairs and a proactive approach which constantly evolves over the years.

To manage tax effectively, you need:

1. The expertise to fully understand and micro manage all of the options available
2. The foresight to overlap strategies so that they interact together to create the desired result
3. The freedom to create an evolving plan over rolling five year timescales
4. A full understanding of the growth patterns of each asset class or fund and the ability to identify the right tax wrapper accordingly
5. The flexibility to move between tax wrappers with no cost or penalty as the shape of returns or tax rules change

So you see tax doesn't need to be so taxing, with careful planning and sound financial advice, investors can develop a robust tax efficient investment strategy which will not only benefit them, but also future generations.

Colin Lawson

NB – figures used are estimates and examples have been simplified. If you are planning to make changes to your investment portfolio speak to a qualified financial adviser.

About the author

Colin is the managing partner of Equilibrium Asset Management; he founded the Wilmslow-based wealth management firm more than 18 years ago. The business has now grown to a team of 30 staff who manage more than £300 million worth of assets for 500 clients.

Equilibrium offers a genuinely personalised financial and investment management service, providing expertise on wealth and investment planning, pensions and inheritance tax strategies from its Wilmslow, Knutsford and Chester offices.

Colin has over 20 years' experience in the financial services market and holds a Diploma in Financial Planning and advanced papers in Personal Investments and Pensions.

In June 2013 Equilibrium was ranked in the top five performing UK wealth management companies in the Financial Times Private Client Wealth Management Survey. It was also named Best Wealth Manager in the UK at the 2013 Money Marketing Awards.

The company also holds New Model Adviser Firm of the Year 2010 (Northern Region); New Breed Adviser Awards Best Pensions, Retirement & Post Retirement Planner 2009; New Breed Adviser Awards Best Paraplanner 2009; Money Management Investing for Income Award 2008 and New Breed Adviser Award Best Support Team 2008.

For more information visit: www.eqllp.co.uk or follow Equilibrium on twitter: @EquilibriumAM

The Mindset Of A Successful Investor

Investing is a bit like having breakfast. Some don't want it, some can't live without it, but if you understand the importance of starting out your day right, and with the right food, it would become an essential part of your health.

So is the mind-set of investing – some don't want it, some can't live without it, but if you understand the importance of changing your thought process, and if you put in the right information into your mind, this will become the most essential part of your wealth.

I know that many people are looking for that 'magic formula' that will turn their world from rags to riches. But the truth is, if you look at some of the most successful people in the world, it is their attitude to life that is more profound than the actual investments they are involved in. So as an introduction, I would like to bring to your attention some of the things I have learned from observing many of my successful clients, as well as listening to famous people who have 'made it'. They all seem to possess -

- A positive outlook in everything they do
- Understanding of their limitations
- A need to build their own 'Success Team'.

Let's break down these points to see if this is relevant for you to becoming a successful investor that you deserve to be.

Positive outlook - Your Attitude:

Is the glass half full or half empty? I have learned that in every situation you can choose to make it good or bad. You will always find someone who will find good in something when you can only see the bad. The truth is, if you look hard enough to find fault, you will always find it. Alternatively, if you want to find good, you can always find good. The successful people almost always turn a negative situation into a positive. They will try to stay positive in any environment, and attract those who also want to be in a positive sphere.

Ask yourself these questions and see if your mind is built to be a successful person –

- Do you take responsibility for your feelings? Or do you blame others for how you feel?

- Do you take responsibility for your actions? Or do you blame others for how you act?
- Do you take responsibility for your thoughts? Or do you blame others for how you think?

So whatever your answer was to the above, try to put yourself in the following situations and go back to the above questions to see if your answers are still the same.

Imagine you are in the following situations –

- Your partner humiliates you in public for one of your nasty habits
- While driving on a freeway, someone is speeding and cuts you off
- Your neighbours' baby cries during the night for 6 hours and you can't sleep
- A work colleague is manipulating your boss's thoughts by boasting about himself, and belittling you.

These are challenging thoughts! However, if you can catch yourself each time you become upset or angry and change the way you respond to a potentially negative situation, I can promise you that your life will look and feel better, and you will start to attract others who want to be positive. Besides, do you know of anyone who wants to be around negative people all the time?

Understanding your Limitations

Many of you already know the statistics on successful people – 5% succeed financially while 95% live a basic life. It is hard to believe that we live in the same world, with the same opportunities and yet only 5% find the 'secret' to success. No use making up excuses and blame our surroundings because there are some who have come from the worst possible circumstances - people such as Nelson Mandela, Oprah Winfrey...I think you get my point.

So what made the difference? I believe that these successful people found out what they were good at, and what they were not so good at.

If you work out what your limitations are, you have a starting point to work from. This is what setting goals is all about.

No goal is attainable if you don't know where to start from, and know where you want to go. A GPS is a great example of understanding your limitations and goal setting – our limitation is that we do not always know how to get to a place, so we can punch in the address and it will point us in the right direction. The GPS however, will require your current address in order to map out a route for you

So if you have limited understanding about finance, you can figure out where you are and where you want to go. A good financial adviser will take your co-ordinates to work out a strategy to get you there as quickly as possible.

If we take the GPS example to the next level, embarking on a major road trip from Sydney to Perth will require a fair bit of planning. Otherwise, you could end up in a harrowing situation. This is the same for investing – careful planning is essential and if you have limited knowledge in wealth creation, the best thing to do is create a plan with a financial adviser before you get started and chances are you will get to your desired goal faster, and with little disruptions along the way.

As for the goal itself, I have found that successful people have an awesome system they follow to achieve them. Yes, they are committed, driven and motivated, but here is a practical approach that if you are not achieving your goals maybe this is something that you should try.

A motivational speaker, Nique stewart from the US, mentioned about a time that he booked in for a 45 minute 'ask any question' session with Sir Richard Branson. When he asked Sir Richard about how he became so successful, his reply was that read his goal card 21 times a day! He will not go to sleep until everything on his goal card was achieved. So the moral of the story is, make goals that are attainable and measurable, keep reminding yourself at every opportunity to keep motivated and complete what you set out to do, no matter how big or small.

Building a Success Team

If you imagine a board meeting and the members have an agenda which sets out the goals they wish to accomplish. They each want to achieve this common goal, and yet their knowledge and expertise are very different from each other. I was taught from a young age that an organisation with a group of people with different opinions will thrive better than having a group of people who are just 'yes' people.

The likelihood of finding a great strategy with many ideas is far better than trying to come up with all the ideas on your own. Hence, the success of an investment venture is far greater if you have a group of experts who are on your side. There are very few single individuals who have made it big just on their own knowledge and strength. To try and do everything yourself will slow you down and may very well hinder your progress towards your goal Almost all successful people have a team of experts that they rely on, and consult with each other on a regular basis.

So why do I mention this? Because your success depends on it. For example, if you are buying your first investment property, you want a good solicitor, mortgage broker and an estate agent. If you decide to go bigger and build a block of units, you need to expand your team to include a builder, engineer, surveyors and so forth. If problems arise, these professionals will use their knowledge and expertise to rectify the situation quickly, so you can keep focusing on the tasks at hand.

Wealthy people understand the benefits of leveraging time and knowledge of others to get to their goal quicker. Doing it all yourself is just too hard. We live in a world where information is changing constantly, and we are seeing more and more people who are becoming specialised in the fields of medicine, law and even finance just to name a few. If you are a keen learner and want to know what would be the best thing to study to build wealth, nothing compares to self – development. If you create a vision of having your own Success Team, your time should be used in learning leadership and negotiation skills.

Leadership and negotiation skills are a fundamental part of life, and yet so few people decide to learn about it. Leadership could mean leading a group of friends on a hiking trip, or being a parent. It could also be leading a small business or a large corporation.

Negotiation skills can also play a big part in your life. I heard someone say that if you are only slightly better a negotiator than a drug dealer, your children will be safe...some have natural talent for negotiating, some have to work hard to learn it, but it still remains to be one of the most important life skills that will help in so many levels of your life.

The first steps towards financial freedom – demystifying the simple facts
The decisions you make today could have a significant impact on your financial future. So let's put some ideas on the table so that you are able to decide on what you should be doing.

Loans: Principal and Interest versus Interest Only – Interest only is a facility that you only pay the interest to the bank. The principal or the original loan amount is not being paid off. This may sound absurd, but there are practical applications that could alter your cashflow, taxation benefits and emergency funding.

If you buy an investment and you borrow money to do so, it is good practice to make this loan into an interest only loan. Reason being is that if you reduce the principal, the amount of interest you pay reduces, so the deductible amount will also reduce over time. So if you have any surplus income you should be focusing on getting rid of personal debts that do not have any interest deductibility, while keeping the investment loan repayments at an absolute minimum. The investment loan can be paid off after all personal debts have been paid off.

100% offset versus Line of Credit – The end result of using your surplus income to reduce debt is exactly the same, but the way in which both of these facilities will change your entire game plan.

A line of credit works exactly like a typical business overdraft – you have a credit limit and you cannot spend over this limit, and often your income will go into this loan to save you interest. For each day that you have your income kept in the loan, the daily interest charge is calculated on the lower outstanding balance.

The 100% offset can accumulate savings, like any other back account. The offset is 'linked' to a loan, so the interest on the loan is calculated by subtracting the accumulated savings from the loan amount, without actually reducing the loan. The offset account will not earn interest, but will be saving interest on the loan.

Choosing between the two will vary according to your situation and what you plan to do. A Line of credit is great if you want to use the funds for investment or business purposes so that you are able to claim interest deductions. An offset account that is connected to an investment loan will mean that the deductible interest will drop and the size of your tax refund would be affected. So this decision making process would involve someone who understands the products and to put the right product in place according to your situation.

Budgeting – I cannot emphasize how important budgeting is to your success – yes, it can be boring, but this information is what tells your current position, and gives you the chance to find out how you are going to achieve your goal.

I am not teaching anything new to you, but it is something that successful people do to measure themselves to see how well they are going. The fundamental rule is that you spend less than you earn.

Get in a habit of taking control of your money. Figure out what you have to send and how much you are going to save. Have a financial adviser do some projections for you with what you could be worth in 10,20,30 years time... once you reach a decision to commit to a specific goal, keep a close eye on your progress – measuring continually will keep you focused and you will soon realise the excitement of contributing towards your 'big picture.

What investment opportunities are out there?

Investment Selection options – There are basically three main sectors that you can invest in – these are property, shares and managed funds, and owning a business. Making a decision on which investments to buy will depend on the priority of the purchase, what your capacity is to service loans, how much deposit you have and what your retirement exit strategy looks like. For example, if you have 2 years to go before retirement, buying an investment property may not suit, but investing in a managed property fund via super may be an alternative.

Another scenario is whether to start your own business or go into investments. If you do not have tools to operate your own business, it would obviously make sense to buy tools first before going into other investments.

The cheapest investment to get into is shares and managed funds. You can choose to invest a ump sum, or gradually build up your investment based on your on monthly savings, or your monthly savings plus borrowings. If you wish to borrow, you can contribute what you can, say $500 per month, and you can borrow another $500 to match your contributions. This means that you can invest a total of $1000 per month to build up your investments.

The next most expensive is property. Most banks require you to save at least 5% of the purchase price, and you also require additional savings to cover for various expenses such as legal fees, stamp duty and mortgage insurance. Some expenses may not apply to you, so it's best to find out what is required for your property transaction.

The most expensive is to buy a business. To buy a McDonalds franchise, you will need about $400,000 to get started. But if you are starting out a new business, you may only need a very small amount to buy a computer, or basic tools of trade to get you started. SO the capital required can vary greatly depending on what you are proposing to do.

The above options for your consideration are quite varied, and the possible outcomes differ greatly, so narrowing down your options is not as easy and should be attempted with someone who can tailor the strategy to suit your unique requirements I would strongly suggest that you discuss your situation with a financial adviser and brain storm all the possibilities first before deciding on an investment strategy.

Craig Richards

About the author

I was born in Japan and lived there till I was 7 years old. My father is Australian an my mother is Japanese, but since my early days were spent in Japan, I came to know and understand the traditions of the Japanese culture – honesty, integrity, persistence, commitment, dedication. Like the kamikaze's who devoted their life to one cause until the last dying breath, I too feel much the same way with regards to the cause I have selected to pursue. To me, this is nothing special, as there are many other Japanese who feel the same way, although I have been told on more than one occasion that this is not normal... regardless of whether this commitment level to life is normal or eccentric, I believe it is important to understand other people's traits, as the journey to succeed in life is founded on these traits.

I have been blessed to be able to do the work I do and the chance to get to know so many people on so many levels, so naturally I want to share something about me in return. I believe that if you can understand why I do what I do, this will help you understand what I wish to share about the things I know in finance - I am not just another broker or planner selling products – I have created something that will change people's lives financially and help people become part of something that the rich people do. My dream is to help every family get out of debt quicker and build their wealth quicker so their retirement will be a happy and prosperous one.

Through the years, my studies have led me to find and create strategies that only the wealthy had access to in the past. With my youngest of memories, my first job was at the age of 5, and by first business venture was at the age of 8. I have always wanted to find out what makes a person rich, and my desire to ensure my own parents would be taken care of financially, I felt such urgency to solve this wealth puzzle before it was too late. I am very happy to say that they are living a comfortable lifestyle today.

My background is in the banking sector, with my final years at the bank as a high net worth bank manager. I wanted to give my clients the best deal, but at the time, I could only sell the prescribed products and not the cheaper interest rate around the corner with another bank. So becoming a mortgage broker solved this issue.

My next challenge was to figure out what investments were available in the market place. I used my previous experience of watching the wealthy clients moving their money around, and I used this platform to further my studies. I became a financial planner and this helped expand the knowledge base considerably.

Over time, I started to merge the complications of loan and investment selection into a more simplified process. I started to create strategies that made a significant difference to clients' debt reduction capabilities and investment opportunities.

Today, we are providing a holistic approach in providing high end professional services for mortgage structuring, financial planning, accounting and selecting appropriate investment solutions to everyone who wish to create true wealth.

Property Investment Is Your Ticket To Freedom

People looking at buying their first investment property often tell me they are concerned it will limit their financial freedom. Nothing could be further from the truth: property investment is a ticket to freedom and one way to ensure you're financially set up for a comfortable retirement. The current market presents ideal conditions for investors, and starting to steadily build up a portfolio gives you a dependable asset and a fantastic, flexible lifestyle; something we're all searching for.

Property is, in my opinion, the best way to achieve real wealth and to ensure you're well set up for your later years. It's solid and relatively easy to understand and is fully supported by a stable government and banking system. This is why you won't see property owners panicking like shareholders might when the market takes a turn for the worse. Property can also be self-funded and provides a passive income, rather than business owners who start their own business to escape from a job, but often end up working twice as hard and only benefit when they sell.

A careful property investment strategy will, overtime, start to provide you with long term rewards and the freedom to focus on doing the things you love with the people that matter most or take some well-deserved time off to travel; all the while knowing you are backed by a bricks-and-mortar asset. Unlike you, your property portfolio is working 24 hours a day, seven days a week to constantly expand your wealth. It took me nine years to gain financial freedom through property investing, by focusing on buying well and steadily building up my portfolio. Once you have one appreciating asset you can build up equity which you use to purchase your next property, without having to fund it from your wages. And that's when the financial benefits allow for a change of lifestyle and, ultimately create freedom.

I believe property is the best possible investment; however the key to getting rewards is to buy well. In over two decades of investing in residential property I have come to believe that "bargain property" is an oxymoron. Everyone wants a bargain, but often bargains are a false economy. The majority of 'bargains' are less desirable properties in less desirable locations that aren't in any great demand. Rather than focussing on finding a cheap deal, you need to know what do to at an auction, or better still before the auction, to ensure you buy your dream home or investment property. Auction day is always very stressful, especially if you have already set your heart on buying. And to make things harder, better homes in better suburbs often sell before auction. So how can you guarantee that you'll secure that perfect property?

Firstly, you need a clear picture of what you are looking for; a defined plan means that you are more likely to find what you want. If you have too many options, you might never make a decision. Once you've found your property, a building inspection is imperative to ensure that there are no hidden problems you will have to repair down the track. You also need a strata inspection when buying a unit and pest inspection when buying a house. These give you a clear idea of any works that you need to add to your budget. It is also vital that you get pre-approved for finance to avoid the frustration of spending months looking for the perfect property, only to have your mortgage application knocked back. If you get pre-approved for finance and tell your bank or mortgage broker the type of property you want to buy, there should be no surprises down the track.

Many in-experienced buyers make emotional decisions when they find their dream property which is why it's important to really do your research, and learn a few tricks of the trade to ensure you're putting your money towards a solid investment. As a professional buyer, I have been buying similar property in the same suburbs for over 10 years and even though I have a good idea of what a property may be worth, I still pay an independent valuer every time I bid. It also helps to get friendly with several property agents as they're the first to be aware of properties for sale. The better you know them, the more likely you will hear about silent sales, as agents often take a property to their closest contacts before the general public. And finally, I strongly encourage you to use a professional buyer. Successful property buyers will look at around 100 properties in the area they are interested in, as well as conduct secondary research, before making a decision. If you're busy, it can be hard to dedicate the time to buying a property. Professionals make the process easier and can help secure a better deal.

So what would a professional buyer recommend? Firstly, rather than trying for undervalued suburbs which may or may not grow, research the market and choose areas that always attract good tenant demand and have scarcity of stock. Property investment professionals always give good ratings to inner urban suburbs such as Melbourne's – Albert Park, Middle Park, St Kilda, Elwood, Elsternwick, Prahran, South Yarra, Armadale, Hawthorn and Sydney's eastern beaches from Maroubra to Bondi Beach, their inner west suburbs such as Leichhardt, Annandale and Balmain and north shore harbour side suburbs including Neutral Bay, Kirribilli and Cremorne.

When done right property truly can be your ticket to freedom, and can lead you into a fun, flexible and exciting retirement. So do some research into the current market and then when you're done, do some more! When you feel confident about your property investment choices, and with the help of professionals go ahead and buy your dream home or investment property, watch its value continue rise and just sit back, relax, and enjoy life!

Chris Gray

About the author

Chris Gray is CEO of Empire which builds property portfolios for other people – searching, negotiating and renovating on their behalf. For clients or to add to his personal portfolio, Chris buys around 1-2 property per week, providing a unique insight into market conditions and buyer and seller sentiment. Chris hosts "Your Property Empire' each Friday on Sky News Business channel, where he interviews various heads of property research and major industry figures. Chris is a qualified accountant, buyers' agent and mortgage broker.

For more information visit www.yourempire.com.au, www.chrisgray.com.au and follow Chris on Twitter: @ChrisGrayEmpire.

The Ten Commandments Of Property Investing

It never ceases to amaze me how few people have a strategy in place for investing in property. This is a trait I have witnessed in those just starting out in the market as well as industry veterans I interview for 'Your Money Your Call' (Fridays on Sky news Business Channel)

When you consider that, for most people, property is the single biggest asset they will purchase; it seems ludicrous to not have a firm strategy in place for investing in it. Whether you are an experienced investor or a novice looking to break into the market, my top ten rules can help you to buy smarter and achieve better returns in the long term. These tips form the backbone of my strategy for Empire clients and for my personal investments:

1. **Choose property that's attractive to tenants**
    Any property you purchase should be in reasonable condition (or able to be upgraded for a reasonable price), have good sized bedrooms, off-street parking and good positioning away from noise and main roads. Look for something that suits the majority of tenants in the area to ensure your property is always attractive to renters. A property that is always tenanted means a stable income stream.

2. **Choose property that will grow in value**
    Properties in locations close to the CBD, leisure facilities, schools, public transport and beaches (where possible) are more likely to gain value in a good market and less likely to lose value in a down market.

3. **Buy blue chip.**
    If a property seems too cheap to be true – it probably is. Cheap properties are cheap for a reason, and that reason is the lack of demand for properties combined with an oversupply in the area. In general, it is worth paying market value for a good property in a top

suburb rather than a property that is cheap because no one really wants it.

4. **Create instant equity through simple renovations.**
    Quick, low-cost renovations such as a paint job, recarpeting, tidying the garden, painting the fence, installing new curtains or blinds and replacing kitchen cupboard doors can have a significant impact on the value of your home. A good rule of thumb is to aim to get back at least $1.00 – 2.00 in value for every dollar you spend on renovations.

5. **Create a buffer by refinancing.**
    When your property has grown in value, it's sensible to create an emergency buffer zone by refinancing. This will ensure you can continue to make mortgage repayments even if unforeseen expenses or loss of income (such as losing your job) occur. Don't find yourself in a forced-sale position, as you won't get the best price and you may have to pay capital gains taxes and other expenses.

6. **Re-sign your tenants.**
    Hire a professional property manager to ensure you get reliable tenants who pay a good market rent. Consider tying your existing tenant down to a new 12-month agreement to help guarantee your rental income.

7. **Get an independent valuation before you buy.**
    Buyers can get emotionally involved when buying property, causing them to pay more than the property is worthy. By investing a few hundred dollars on an independent valuation, you can almost guarantee you will never pay too much.

8. **You don't have to sell to profit.**
   Don't think you need to sell to realise capital growth gained in a property. Selling a property incurs sales costs and taxes and, often, re-buying costs. By refinancing you have access to profits made on the property while holding on to your asset. This is similar to a reverse mortgage.

9. **Property investing is all about time in the market.**
   Timing the market is for speculators not investors. If you can afford to buy and hold on to your asset, the time is right to buy.

And my most important tip:

10. **Build a team of professional advisors.**
    You can't do everything yourself. An initial outlay for hiring professionals who are experts in their field can make a difference of tens of thousands of dollars to your long term returns. As a starting point, every investor should have an accountant, mortgage broker, financial advisor, valuer, building inspector and buyers' agent. There are companies who will organise all of this for you. For instance, at Empire, we build property portfolios for time poor professionals and we have built up a whole network of contacts who are the best in their field and bale to make your property investment a success.

Chris Gray

Why You're Better Off Ringside – The Perils Of Going It Alone In Property

A few years ago I travelled to Thailand with a good friend of mine. For one of the first trips out of the country, we had a blast.

One of our funniest memories was going to a kickboxing tournament in Bangkok where some of the young kids would go through their paces in front of a crowd of jeering tourists. As the night wore on, they would invite daring participants up on the stage to see if they had 'the metal'. Without doubt, some drunken lad whose enthusiasm failed to match his talent proceeded to have himself upended by a young Thai boxer who had been reserving himself for the final round with a tourist.

That's when I learnt to respect the professionals.

Michael Jordan. Henry Ford. Harry Seidler. All great professionals in their own field. They worked hard. They studied and practised in their field of expertise every day. They were coached on the nuances that made them stand out from the crowd.

But they were the Greats. Let's take a look at something a little closer to home.

My accountant; a consummate professional. Last year my accountant charged me $10,000 to do my tax, God love him. He ended up saving me $70,000 in that financial year. Worth every penny.

Could I have done that tax return myself? Yes. Would I have achieved the same result? Not nearly. And why? Because I don't know tax like he does and I can't 'read between the numbers' like he can.

Of course, we don't need a professional for every occasion. Driving a car, doing the shopping, picking up the kids from school (although that would help) do not require professionals. Professionals emerge only when there's a lot at stake or there's a large reward. It's quite acceptable to be an amateur at the mundane.

It pains me to see people who risk so much, work so hard and then front up to the real estate market to make one of the largest financial purchases they will ever make in their life, and then decide to go it alone. To add insult to injury, the parties then enter into a 'negotiation' where the mediator works for the seller. Hardly an impartial influence!

I would be lying if I said I wasn't trying to show you the benefit of using a Buyers' Agent in the market. But I do believe in what I do. The relationships we have in this industry, the market knowledge and the financial know-how - it truly is an unfair advantage against those buyers looking to pit themselves against the professionals in the ring every day.

So the next time you decide to make a move in the market, ask yourself whether you have what it takes. Purchasing property will most likely be one of the biggest financial decisions you will make in your life and you would be wise to have someone in your corner, who knows the game and is an expert in their field.

Chris Gray

Positive Income Generators

Nearly all of us have heard from our parents, that to 'make it' we need to be really well educated. Make the most of school, do our best, head to college and work the corporate 9 to 5 to really get ahead.

Yet, there seems to be a huge shift of late with enormously successful people who truly just don't fit the mould. Big disruptors are out there, who have never had a college education, yet overcome the odds and are turning all that thinking on its head! Richard Branson, Oprah Winfrey and Steve Jobs are all examples. It's often their originality or 'thinking outside the box' that got them started on the road to super-success in the first place. And the old chestnut 'Never Give Up!'

And although most of us don't aspire to the dizzying heights of being a billionaire, a bit more income is usually welcome, especially when we don't have to work too hard for it.

One thing that many have in common is a rather entrepreneurial spirit, a 'can-do' attitude and the ability to build businesses that don't always rely on them to be working 'in them.'

Having the resources to build an income that continues to flow, passively if possible, is the goal of many. And in theory, it sounds great! But for those who've never put themselves out there, stepped out of the safety of a 9-5, how can it work? And what's available to get started in PIG (Positive / Passive Income Generators) farming?

These days, most peoples' thoughts turn to on-line options... so here's a couple of ways to get started:

- Blogging
- Affiliate Marketing

- Direct Selling
- Surveys
- Property
- Investing
- Purchasing a Business

A little more on each of those shortly…

I've actually chosen very deliberately, to use the word *Positive* Income Generators, as in truth, there's very little available in the *Passive* Income Generator space.

'Passive' to me, means sitting on your backside and waiting for the dollars to flow in and if you've found the secret to that, let me know! Aside from a wisely invested windfall, most passive and positive income generators, still start with a bit of work.

Blogging requires time, even if you outsource, you'll need to come up with the idea – and maybe pay for someone to put the articles together. Affiliate marketing means setting up relationships – also taking time. Direct selling can mean lots of time; with party plan selling requiring much in set up and delivery and taking the time to get to know people, forge friendships and build rapport. Websites require setup, upfront fees and monitoring, surveys take time, property investments require due diligence and research, as does purchasing a business.

Nothing in this chapter requires sitting back with your feet on the desk and waiting for the dollars to start flowing, so as long as you're prepared to put in some 'elbow grease,' time or effort to start with, the money can follow. So, is the payoff worth it? Of course!

My top tip is still to invest in yourself first. Whichever of the PIGs appeal most to you, the best favour you can do for yourself is to learn all you can about it. Whether that means taking a course, trawling on-line articles, reading books, attending lectures and information nights, or picking the brains of people successful in that field – get started. It's never a wasted moment to invest in your own education.

As Benjamin Franklin best put it, "An investment in knowledge pays the best interest."

And before we get into the options, there's lots of people out there looking to part you from your hard earned cash rather than help you increase it… so do look out for:

- Get Rich Quick schemes – remember, if it sounds too good to be true, it usually is!
- Systems that seem a little 'ad-hoc' – usually a tried a tested, proven formula needs to be at work
- Offers that insist you don't need to learn a thing! A legitimate system will want you to learn all about it, how it works and where the revenue comes from. A method that insists you don't need to spend any time on learning is likely a scam – you'll always need to take the time to ensure you explore details and understand the system

So, a little more on each of the mentioned PIGS and how they can possibly work for you.

Blogging

We've seen or heard the stories; great blog gets picked up and made into next Hollywood blockbuster... think *Julie & Julia*. And if you're a tortured writer, this may be the avenue for you.

Most blogs start with an idea, something that you're interested in or passionate about, but that doesn't need to be the case. The trouble with you being the expert blogger, creating a niche market and getting tons of readers, still means, that "you are the business" and there's nothing passive about that. You stop writing on the topic and you're stuck, because you've made it all about you. Selling your site later can be an issue, because if you're no longer writing the content, the value drops.

If you do choose blogging, you need to understand that it has to become a business asset for you. That means your *Killer Content* gets *Heaps of Traffic*, leading to *Loads of Cash*.

A great idea is to find the BIG areas on the net that people are interested in – off the top of my head, Finance, Business, Travel, Food & Wine, Gaming, Weight Loss and Animals/Pets come to mind. Yes, these are already huge and well covered areas, but what that also means is, lots of people want to read about it and lots of people would be willing to write about it too.

So, once you've figured out what you want to blog about – get writers to help you out. There's lots out there with great ideas who love writing, but don't have much exposure. Sites such as sourcebottle.com, myblogguest.com and blogSynergy.com are available to help out. Research sites that put together guest bloggers and see how all the writers contribute different stories to the overall whole, in turn creating great content all brought together, without you having to write a word (unless you really want to!)

This book is an example of how it works. The publisher has called for writers to contribute, each who shares their expertise; they'll probably not know each other or ever meet, even are continents apart, but are managed as a cohesive whole into a saleable asset – the book you're now reading. And that's what you're aiming to achieve with your blog.

Once you've got the site and writers sorted, you need people to find your site. That's called Traffic. Social Media (SM) has lots of tools for you to increase the word about what you have, and there's even sites who'll manage this for you for a very low cost. Check out sites like microworkers.com or fiverr.com to see what's available. The writers also want to be seen and will be more than happy to share the articles via their own SM channels too, in turn increasing traffic to your site further.

As a sideline, if you're interested in photography and have the ability to take some great pics, a further income can be derived from adding your pictures to stock image websites. Lots of marketers and companies look for royalty free photographs to include in their projects.

So, you've got the rocking content and the traffic is flowing, now people will want to advertise on your site, you can be found in google, start selling via your site and profits will be more likely to start flowing! Check out Affiliate marketing for how to cash in further on your Blog.

Affiliate Marketing

Affiliate marketing relies on you offering financial incentives to drive sales in lieu of the more traditional referral marketing based on trust and personal relationships.

Your business, the 'Merchant' will reward 'Affiliates' for each new visitor or customer brought in by the affiliate's efforts, clients you otherwise would not have had. Almost like a profit-share.

For Merchants, or those with something to sell, affiliate marketing builds your own online sales team and drives customers to various sites without high advertising costs.

For Affiliates, there's the opportunity to earn good income from your site or blog, while providing related services to your visitors.

This works extremely well for online businesses as it is a form of internet marketing where 'The Merchant' pays 'Affiliates' for generating sales. Clients may click on banner advertising you have and complete a sale, never having previously seen your site.

As an example, you may have a business that aims at raising financial literacy for women by selling webinars or downloads. You are then the Merchant. You, in turn, set up relationships with those who have databases also targeted at women; perhaps a clothing retailer, make-up sales channel or a women's inspiration site. For every client that comes through one of the traceable channels of your Affiliate, a share of the funds or a commission goes to them for the business that's come in.

Alternately, if you as a Merchant sell physical products such as Pet food, you may form affiliate relationships with local vets or sites that blog about animals to increase sales.

If you choose instead to be the Affiliate because you have a Blog with great traffic, you'll get a share of each sale made generated by your site.

These methods are often referred to as Cost Per Sale, Cost Per Lead or Cost Per Click. Whichever way they come, the Affiliate has done the work for the Merchant. Sites such as clixGalore.com are global providers who can assist in setting up what you need.

That's what I call "Win, Win Marketing!"

You may have heard of PPC or Paid Per Click (PPC) Advertising before. And it's a really good idea to have a proper working knowledge of all the keywords and how the market works to earn really good money from PPC. Those who know how to do it, and do it well and make serious gains from their campaigns. This isn't always possible or likely for newbies.

Direct Selling

Direct Selling has been around forever! Think of the early days of the travelling salesman walking from home to home, city to city touting his wares. These days, think Tupperware, Avon, Arbonne.

It occurs when an independent sales consultant sells you goods or services directly, either in your home, work place or a selected meeting area, rather than the traditional retail store. Often 'party plan' sales or demonstrations are involved.

Some of the benefits of purchasing this way means you get to see the products at work before you buy, you can test them for yourself and the consultant can tailor the demonstration to suit what you and your friends would be most interested in. The consultations take place in a relaxed and friendly environment with flexible timing. The goods are delivered to your door and you have the right to cancel orders within given time frames. Purchases are guaranteed and you have a direct personal relationship with the seller and usually, ongoing after sales service.

Be sure, if researching Direct Selling options that first, you truly believe in the products, love and use them yourself; and that secondly, you avoid Pyramid Schemes. These are illegal in some countries. Pyramid schemes seek to generate their income from those who participate in the form of recruiting others. True direct selling companies rely on solid sales revenue over a period of time. Find a company who's stood the test of time, and has a great base of customers who love and use the product. Multi-level marketing (MLM) structures are still commonly used in the direct selling industry but differ from pyramid schemes. A big tell-tale sign is likely to be a large upfront payment being required for overpriced products whereas direct selling rewards the sale of products and services to consumers. Legitimate companies are also likely to be members of national Direct Selling Associations.

So far not sounding terribly 'passive' right? Right! Not to start with anyway...

The true benefits come when you start reaping the rewards of sales by your recruits, also referred to as 'down lines.'

Quality direct selling organisations will usually invest in training its salespeople and help you get started in business. Make sure you understand the reward structure. And be aware, that the amount of time required to be successful can vary. If your goal is to personally rely on the income from the sales, this can take time and is not considered 'passive income.' Having a great team of recruits of 'down lines' working on your behalf is where the passive or positive income can be earned.

Taking the time to train and develop a great team of direct sellers is however, a way some companies allow you to earn further dollars without sticking to the sales routine personally. You will still need to manage your team of recruits, set goals and invest time to work on direct selling activities. Some very successful entrepreneurs earn up to $250k per month from their activities!

Direct selling is certainly not for everyone, but for those who really invest in it, it can be hugely successful.

Surveys

Although not to be considered 'passive income,' completing surveys can still complement your existing income and will certainly generate 'positive income' with the investment usually of just your time and opinion.

And most of us aren't backwards in coming forwards when actually asked what we really think!

Many surveys can be done whilst winding down for bed for the night or watching TV in the evening.

Usually, you'll need to sign up with an online paid survey site and complete a member profile – which details either a little or a lot about you. Then, when a survey matches your profiles, you'll receive an email to complete the survey within a specified time frame.

Making a few dollars with the click of a mouse or completing some questions isn't too painstaking and will supplement your income to either pay down debt or be 'fun money.' Some are as simple as clicking on a link; others can take up to 45 minutes to go through a questionnaire. The rewards can vary from 5c per click to $50. On average, you're looking at around 15-20 minutes for an average length survey, which can decrease as your skills improve.

It's all about the time you're prepared to invest and whether you feel it's worth it.

Lots of companies are looking for feedback on their products or services before releasing them to market and are prepared to pay for your honest contributions.

Googling 'paid surveys' will give you options but look in your particular area, as some survey sites only want citizens of their particular country contributing. Check out the rewards program for each to see if it's how you want to be remunerated, some pay in points that need to be converted, others with gift vouchers and some with goods or cash. The choice is yours. Again, do your homework.

And yes, there are survey scams out there too. Avoid any company that wants you to:

1. pay a membership fee,
2. promises a set income,
3. is not perfectly clear on how your remunerated or

4. asks for overly personal information like bank account details or social security number.

Property

So, this topic on its own has been the subject of many, many books. Now to condense it!

Direct Property investing can be positively, negatively or neutrally geared.

Positively geared means the income received outweighs the costs involved in owing the property and this is what most people want. Negatively geared means the difference comes out of your pocket and unless you have large tax liabilities, good cash flow or potential capital gains, should probably be avoided by most. Neutral gearing means it looks after itself and neither costs you anything or provides much of an income.

Property can take the form of residential, commercial, retail or industrial spaces, but the principles are all the same. You own the land and/or building, and someone pays you an income or rent to use the space and you take care of the costs of ownership; usually interest on borrowings, insurance, taxes, rates, some utilities and duties.

Like any investment opportunity, property isn't for everyone, and it's worth sitting down with your Financial Adviser to see if this option should be included in your portfolio.

Some have been able to use the passive income from property over time to completely replace their 'earned income.'

If you can't afford to service an expensive loan, you need the rent to be able to take care of mortgage payments for you. Generally speaking, property prices rise over the long term, meaning that block of land that your grandparents bought fifty years ago, is likely to cost a lot more today. That's called a 'capital gain' and is only realised when you sell the property. This is very different to generating an ongoing positive income from property. Although properties that do both, are what you're really after.

As an example, you might find a property worth $350k (including purchase costs.) You've saved a deposit of $35k (10%) and are pretty sure you'll get around $400 per week for rent. Let's do the sums:

Interest on Loan - $350k- $35k = $315k @ 5% p/a Interest = $15 750

Annual Land & Water Rates $ 2 000

Insurance on Building & Fittings $ 1 000
_____$18 750

Rental Income @ $400 p/week
                        $20 800

On the surface, it appears you have yourself a positively geared property. But always prepare for a period where no rent may be paid – of up to 4 weeks per year which could take $1600 from the difference. You'll also need to decide whether you're going to manage the investment yourself, or put professional property managers in place, who generally take around 8% of the income, plus a couple of weeks rent per annum. This can further eat into the difference, but they can also be worth their weight in gold if you get a good one!

Lots of variables can change to give a different scenario. What if interest rates move? Will the cost of insurance remain the same? Are you able to increase the rent every six months and keep tenants? Should you pay extra for insurance in case tenants damage the property? Can you afford to tip a bit in if something untoward occurs? Can you afford maintenance if something goes wrong? Is the property older and likely to require work? Did you invest in a Building Inspection? There's a lot to consider with property and due diligence is required.

Negatively geared properties are easy to find. Even professionals will tell you it's easy to lose money on an investment. Making money on investments is a different story. Naturally, most people want positively geared properties, they're in higher demand and this can in turn, raise the price. Do your research on what to look for.

Talk to friends and family who've done it *successfully* before and ask questions. If things went 'pear-shaped' ask what went wrong, could it have been avoided, and what would they do differently or learn from the experience. That can save you a lot of heartache by 'having to learn the hard way' and always seek professional advice.

Advisers and Accountants can help you work out the best ownership structure, how to best use the income, give the pros and cons of various investments, and where possible, legally minimise taxation.

Maybe you can't afford a deposit and could invest in a property unit trust in the meantime, whilst building your nest egg. You may pay a small percentage in management costs instead, but be exposed to a large range of properties you'd never otherwise have access too – without any day to day involvement or management burdens!

Investing

Most investments offer the potential to increase the value your savings over time. We either invest for long-term capital growth or income from our funds, sometimes both.

We've all heard, 'the higher the risk, the higher the return' and although not always true, the saying implies that often riskier investments offer the potential of higher rewards. Some people are born gamblers and happy to 'take a punt' with their investment savings on the likelihood of a huge payoff. They're also more likely to be caught by High-Yield Investment Programs (HYIP) or Ponzi schemes.   Others are extremely conservative, never venturing outside cash and term deposits, believe every horror story they've ever heard on dodgy investments, and believe slow and steady really does win the race. Some believe it all comes down to Fear Vs Greed.

Our personal beliefs, in jargon, are called our Investment Profiles and need to be taken into consideration when we invest. Any adviser who offers a 'cookie cutter' approach or that all clients get the same strategy is investing to their own risk profile and not their clients. I often refer to this as 'the sleep at night' test.   Will you be comfortable enough with the recommendations made to sleep easily at night depending on what you've heard on the news that evening?

As an example, we've recently been through what's been termed a global recession or global financial crisis (GFC.) Are you invested for the very long term and happy to ride out any of the serious 'dips,' prolonged or otherwise; will you want to react quickly to market movements, or will your imminent retirement be affected if you don't respond and make the needed changes?

Seeing we're all different, a personal approach is required with investing. We can choose to go it alone, being a true DIY Investor that trusts our gut or training, or trust that someone who's spent years in the industry may have the nous to serve our needs better, especially if their livelihood depends on it.

Whether we include managed funds (where professionals manage our money on our behalf, for a fee) or directly invest in shares by picking our favourite companies (for the cost of the brokerage) all can have a place if our comfort levels allow.

Seeking professional help may mean access to other investments that individual consumers may not otherwise have access to, and paying for professional advice may not just result in a strategy that suits, takes care of taxation and ownership issues, estate planning and legacy concerns and improve our overall situation in unexpected ways.

I'd suggest that if you've never used an Adviser before, talk to some friends who have. See if they know, like and trust the person they're using. In this age of social media, many have blogs, use Twitter or Facebook, and have websites or YouTube channels so you can know whether you'd be comfortable using a particular firm, before you even pick up the phone. Many will offer their initial consultation at their own expense and own time. Use this time to ask questions you have, discuss fees and how they operate. Ask for referrals, check that they belong to professional bodies and their qualifications.

Choosing an Adviser is a personal decision and requires great care as you're going to be financially intimate with this person. It's worth taking time to get it right.

Buying a Business

If funds allow, another way to generate income is to purchase an established business and the first step is to analyse the advantages and disadvantages of the potential investment.

A good business history may indicate a successful operation and assist when applying for finance where needed. Overstating the goodwill figure in the business, along with a poor reputation from existing management and staff and hurt future prospects.

So, if you have no idea how to read financials, enlist the help of someone who can! Usually a solicitor, accountant or business adviser will have the necessary credentials.

They will need to consider the following before offering a recommendation to purchase or run!

- Vendor – what is the reason for sale of business? Approaching retirement or drop in profits?
- Sales – this includes patterns, trends, customer base, and current suppliers. Has a new competitor opened nearby whose cornered the market? Is there a strong existing loyalty to the business?
- Costs – these cover both the fixed and variable costs to the business and include staff costs too.
- Profits - analyse existing financial records, historical figures, future cash flow and profitability
- Assets - identify and check all assets, including physical and intellectual property and leasing arrangements
- Liabilities – are there many outstanding debts? What are the refund and warranties policies?
- Purchase agreement - review carefully! Always get professional help to review the contract!
- Tax - are there GST, Capital Gains Tax or stamp duty implications on purchase?

- Check Legal issues – what existing leases are there, what's the business structure, do you get the keep the trading name, and do you want to?

There's a lot to consider when purchasing a business and depending on the reason for sale and existing business statistics, can represent good future income. Some businesses sell for a multiple of their annual earnings, and can be picked up for around one time (or less) of their usual annual income.

Aside from the business considerations, evaluate your own skill set. Have you ever run a business? Do you know what you're doing? Do you have something unique you can bring to the business to further increase its sales potential? As an example, a clothing retailer may be successful in its current street address, but has never considered an online store or social media marketing, which you'd have no trouble in setting up. Could this be an advantage? Are the existing staff and asset or need to go? If you don't have the required skill set, can you place a great manager into the business and still turn a profit?

So, I've only considered a few options in this chapter.

I'm sure as you've read you may have thought of others and will tell me there's plenty more I've left out.

Starting your own business for one; becoming a mystery shopper; selling online via methods such as EBay or Etsy; owning ATMs or vending machines; content writing; sports betting; freelance work or franchising existing businesses are other methods, all of which have the potential to add to your income, when done well.

Yes, there are literally hundreds of methods to setup "passive income sources" in a way that means income can flow with little supervision. But hopefully, these few options have at least inspired you to take in interest in what's available, do a bit more research and see if you can create your own ways of making some extra dollars.

Once you've got the idea and have started working it, remember that it's all part of a bigger plan.

All ideas need to be managed in part, with a spot of frugality, making the most of what you have, living within your means and being willing to take advantage of opportunities. It doesn't mean you can immediately walk away from the 9-5, but by taking the steps to set things up now, you're on your way.

If times are tough and the extra income is all about getting out of debt, maybe start with learning how to make the most of what you already have, research websites or blogs that promote savings and frugal living. Then, future earnings will be cream!

I'd always recommend to chat to an adviser about what's best to do with the extra income earned. Should it go to reduce excess debt? Be put towards retirement savings? Pay down the house? Set aside for kids' education? Invest in better insurance protection or investment funds?

All areas require consideration and a professional can help work out what's the best strategy for you.

Amanda Cassar

About the author

Amanda Cassar is a Financial Adviser based on the Gold Coast of Australia, living with her husband and two teenage children and you'll often their friends also running tame throughout the family home with a cat, dog, turtles and fish thrown in also. She runs a successful financial planning practice, Wealth Planning Partners and is involved in a new venture to encourage female empowerment around money, called Financially Fabulous. She has been in the financial services industry since leaving high-school and enjoys travelling throughout Australia to assist her clients.

Amanda has a Masters Degree in Financial Planning and loves assisting her clients set and attain their goals too, with protection strategies for their existing wealth, plans on how to best manage within our means, and still retire in style.

With an appetite for good food, great wine, the company of friends, diving and travel, she works to indulge in her passions and live a great lifestyle. Amanda can be found on Twitter @WealthPP and @financechicks and on LinkedIn if you'd like to connect with her.

How Long Is A Piece Of String? Creating Wealth For Your Retirement

"If you don't design your own life plan, chances are you'll fall into someone else's plan. And guess what they have planned for you? Not much" Jim Rohn.

When do you start thinking about your future retirement plans yet?
How much is enough to retire on?
How do I build the wealth I need before I retire?
These questions are a bit like asking, "How long is a piece of string"!
I wish I had a dollar for every time these questions are asked. I get asked these questions on a daily basis whether it is clients, my radio listeners, seminar attendees or family and friends; these are a few questions that everyone would love to have an exact answer too.

"How much is enough to retire on" or "How do I build the wealth I need before I retire"?

Guess what – unfortunately, there is no one amount that works for everyone. I wish there was a magical answer but unfortunately there isn't, what might be right for one person's circumstances may not be for another. However, planning and various projections can be tailored to your needs; this will certainly go a long way towards helping to source an answer. The answer will vary according to each person's goals, objectives and expectations. An individual's expectation of life style, personal and financial circumstances, and retirement plans can differ enormously.

Planning for the comfortable retirement you deserve needs an honest and tough look at your current circumstances so that you can realistically work towards your retirement goals. You must consider your wages, household budget, current level of spending and your debts.

Do not wait until tomorrow, start your planning today. Do not count on a financial windfall, like an inheritance, that may come your way or for your numbers to come up via a tattslotto jackpot. There is no time like the present to start thinking about various strategies for wealth creation for your retirement, and more importantly, implementing your plan.

I believe that there are some guidelines around which an answer could be formulated; firstly, there are Five Foundation questions that need to be answered so you can truly understand your retirement needs.

The Five Foundation Questions

1. At what age do you want to retire?

This is extremely important, as the earlier you are considering retirement, the earlier you need to be contributing and the more aggressive your wealth creation planning will need to be. Your retirement age will have a major impact upon planning decisions, as it will help determine how long your accumulated wealth will most likely last. I have seen so many cases where people have retired too early if life and have run out of money too early into their retirement. When making your retirement age decision, you must take into consideration that we are expected to live a lot longer with the advancements in both medicine and technology.

2. Where will you live when you're retired?

Along with you're expected age of retirement, where you will live when you retire will also have a major impact on your wealth creation plan. Consider the costs of living that will vary greatly depending on your decision; whether it is by the sea or the country, metropolitan areas or city center, in a purpose built retirement facility or independent living. The result of your decision can have a substantial effect on your retirement costs and how long your accumulated money will actually last.

3. What will you do with your time?

Again, dependent upon the lifestyle you would like to live in retirement, it will impact the amount of money you will require. For example, if you plan to travel the world, it will be a lot more expensive when compared to living in a country cottage living a simple life. Expenses to consider are travelling/holiday costs, expensive memberships (e.g. golf or gym memberships), and large family events, like weddings.

4. How much money will you need?

The money needed to retire in comfort will vary for each person based upon their individual circumstances, along with their expectations also. You will need to consider what does it cost you to live today and how will I create that cash flow in retirement? Maybe a practice retirement period could be something that you trial to see how much it will actually cost, and more importantly, whether you actually enjoy being retired.

5. Where will the money come from?

In retirement, your monies will need to come from the wealth you have accumulated throughout your working years. However with guidance from your accountant and financial advisor this wealth can continue to accumulate in passive incomes depending on the investments made with your retirement fund. Sources of passive income can be found in rental properties, dividends from shares, or interest from savings accounts. Your source of investment and passive income will vary depending on how aggressive your wealth creation plan is and is best discussed with your financial advisor.

Thinking about these questions along with others will give you a starting point and probably lead to more questions; however with these Five Foundation questions you can kick start the task of planning how to accumulate wealth for your retirement.

Be sure to check that your superannuation fund is performing at above average standards and that your investment mix is something that you're very comfortable with. Seek the help of a proactive accountant if you are like most that gets totally confused about superannuation. We are also here to help where we can.

The Figures
If you are unsure where to start I suggest that to achieve comfortable lifestyle in retirement, retirees should aim for an annual income amounting to at least 70 to 80 per cent of their final salary.

I prefer use net (after-tax or 'cash in hand') income, as this is what you have been used to living on. I suggest that it would be ideal to retire on 75 per cent or more of your final "net" pay. In other words, if your family were currently receiving an annual after-tax income of $100,000 while working, then an after-tax retirement annual income of $75,000 would be more than appropriate in retirement, and would certainly be a fantastic starting point. Annual Income ÷ 75% = Annual Retirement Income Required

A couple retiring when they both reach 65 years of age, based upon the current life expectancy table, will require about $1.2 million in superannuation monies. This will provide a tax-free pension beginning at $75,000 per year and then being indexed at 2 per cent annually to help partially keep up with inflation.

In reading this, most of you are probably saying how can we possibly accumulate 1.2 million dollars in our superannuation fund – there is just no way no matter what we do? Your right, if you keep telling yourself that, you probably won't, but if you start acting on your plan to create wealth you will be surprised at what you can possibly achieve.

There is certainly nothing wrong with having a go. Start contributing a little each week or each month as early in life as possible, and you may just surprise yourself. There is certainly no excuse for the younger generation these days as they have the added benefit of compulsory superannuation contributions from their employment from day one. This is a great advantage when compared to previous generations whom didn't have this added benefit.

In simple terms, the earlier you start a savings plan and accumulating wealth, the easier it will be and the more comfortable it will be later on in life!

Accumulating wealth inside of your superannuation is pretty simple; picture it very similar to paying off your mortgage or home loan. With a mortgage, we borrow and spend the whole amount on the purchase of a home. Over time, on top of the minimum repayment per month, we tip extra against our mortgage to help us repay it as quickly as possible, and along the way saving us tens of thousands of dollars in both interest and charges.

As suggested, saving for our retirement through superannuation is a very similar concept. In many countries our employers are required by law to contribute the minimum payment into our superannuation fund depending on our level of gross wages. Please do not rely or presume that this will be anywhere near enough for your retirement years – trust me, it won't even be close!

One question to ask yourself, what can you afford to contribute on top of this amount; even if it is a small amount per week or per month. Over the years, these extra contributions will continue to grow and accumulate to give you a lot more comfort in retirement – something that we all deserve.

Thinking about these questions along with others will give you a starting point and probably lead to more questions, but at least you can start getting the help you may require and begin the task of accumulating wealth for your retirement.

Case Study - Salary Sacrificing

Cynthia is 30 years of age and decides that she would like to salary sacrifice an extra $100 per week into her superannuation fund to help her reach financial freedom in retirement. It is estimated that over the next 30 years, this will earn 6 percent on average in earnings per annum. The big question, how much extra will Cynthia have available at age 60.

Table One

	Opening Balance	Contribution (Per Annum)	Earnings	Closing Balance
Year 1	$ -	$5,200	$312	$5,512
Year 2	$5,512	$5,200	$643	$11,355
Year 5	$24,113	$5,200	$1,759	$31,072
Year 10	$63,340	$5,200	$4,112	$72,653

Year 15	$115,835	$5,200	$7,262	$128,297
Year 20	$186,085	$5,200	$11,477	$202,762
Year 30	$405,903	$5,200	$24,666	$435,769

As you see in Table One, by Cynthia tipping in an extra $100 per week over the next 30 years, along with her subsequent earnings added to this, Cynthia saves the an amount of $435,769 inside superannuation. A fantastic result, using a very simple strategy. This will be added to her compulsory employer contributions over her working life year and would definitely result in a great starting point when her retirement rolls around.

Cynthia would achieve financial freedom in retirement with this simple, yet consistent strategy.

Another important item for consideration; Do you actually understand how your superannuation is performing? This is the one area where almost everyone let's himself or herself down. Are you the type of person that doesn't know how much you have in superannuation, how your superannuation fund is actually performing or even whether your employer is contributing the correct amount required by law? Reviewing your superannuation is quite simple ask yourself these questions; could it perform better in an alternative retail or industry fund, or will utilising a Self-Managed Superannuation Fund (SMSF) give you greater results? It is predicted that SMSF's will continue to grow and become the most popular vehicles for retirees by far. If you have trouble understanding your superannuation statement, then get clarification or seek the help from someone that can help.

As we do with our mortgages, you must also "compare and analyse your superannuation fund". Even the smallest of adjustments earlier on in your life can make a massive difference by the time you reach your 60's when you need as much as possible in your superannuation for retirement. Although those that are younger in age will do better in the future years, as they will have the benefit of the superannuation guarantee for the whole of their working lives, they will most likely still struggle to afford a comfortable retirement without additional input and strategies.

Never ever underestimate how much one needs in retirement! You don't know what is just around the corner".
Start as early as possible in life accumulating wealth, there is no right time or right amount; you may just surprise yourself with how much you can actually save! Social security and age pensions might not support you fully in the future, so the sooner you begin saving and investing, the financial security you have in retirement will be greater.

We all want choices and flexibility in retirement; the earlier we address the issues that we need to consider, the more likely the chance of achieving financial security in retirement.

Peter Locandro

About the author

Peter Locandro is a CPA qualified accountant with over 20 years public practice experience based out of Melbourne, Australia. As Principal accountant of his business ZJL Partners, Peter and his team service over 4,000 clients and have won the prestigious "Accountancy Business of the Year" awarded by the Proactive Accountants Network in both 2012 and 2013.

Peter is an accountant who is about more than just the numbers. He is also a public speaker, radio host, blogger, marathon runner and small business mentor. He has featured in Australian national newspapers The Sydney Morning Herald Newspaper and The Age 'Money' as well as local publications 'The Stakeholder' and 'Our Town'.

Unlike many accountants Peter focuses proactively on educating his clients to understand their financial situation and empowers them with the tools to create wealth for their retirement. Peter specialises in Self Managed Superannuation Funds (SMSF) and transitioning to retirement plans. He has developed the "Running Accountant Theory" which breaks down the taxation saving strategies and wealth creation methods that are used to retire in comfort into easy to understand terminology.

His expertises have lead to public speaking engagements with many Australian business institutions, including; Westpac Bank, The Bank of Melbourne, Ray White Real Estate, Eview Real Estate, Rotary Club of Victoria.

More information about Peter and his work can be found on his business website www.zjl.com.au and his personal blog www.therunningaccountant.wordpress.com.

Avoiding Fears Is Stronger Than Achieving Goals

Financial freedom is different for everyone. For some people it is to leave at a moment's notice on a private jet to the Bahamas. For some it's to turn up to work 2 days a week, and for others it is surviving on a self-sustaining farm by only eating the food produced at home. The people who follow these paths all consider their respective choice as financial freedom, and none are better or more noble then the other.

I believe achieving financial freedom is within everyone's grasp – you just have to identify it first. And that is your job. You figure out what you want, and I'll help you get there. Fair deal? Okay, let's go……

If you haven't already figured out what you want from life, a great place to start is with the end in mind….. your last days. I know, I know. Not a great topic, but let's remove ourselves from the connotations and simply accept for a second that this moment in time will exist.

What do you want from that moment? Do you want regret of things you have done? Things you haven't done? Will you be in a government age facility, or with family at home? None of this is a pretty picture, but I want you to understand where you will end up, because this will determine your course. If you don't know where you will end up, then you don't know where you are headed, and if you don't know where you are headed, you have nothing to aim for. And with nothing to aim for, you end up with exactly that – nothing. More than anything I want you to first know what you want from life, and if you haven't done this yet, using your final days is the best way I know how to jolt your mind into action. Let me explain.

Physiologically humans will choose to avoid a bad situation rather than to attempt to gain pleasure. Fear is a certainty to avoid, goals are just a nice thing that may happen, and for that reason I like people to identify what they want to avoid first. For example if you are inside a burning building, that passion – to avoid death – will be stronger than any plans you will ever make to go on a holiday to Bali.

Bali is a nice idea. Bali would be good. I can one day enjoy Bali. It's ultimately a passive idea, as in, if you don't get to Bali it's not the end of the world. It's just 'well, I might get to Bali next year'.

But if you're inside a burning building, surrounded on all four sides by fire, you're lungs are filling with smoke and your eyes are burning, well 'I'll get to Bali one day' is the last thing on your mind. At that point in time you don't give a hoot about going to Bali. Bali is now a horrible idea. Bali is stupid. Bali can keep it's cheap watches and hired mopeds.

Point is, there is only one thing on your mind – get out of harms way. And you will never be more motivated than this point in your life. You have to get out of the fire. This is the only option.

Avoiding fears is stronger than achieving goals.

That's why I want you to understand that if you do not start this process with the end in mind, you will end up in a place you don't want to be.

Notwithstanding the importance of staring at your own demise in the face, it's certainly time now to focus on the much more desirable side of the equation – what to do with your life! Because ultimately financial freedom will allow you to pursue what you want out of life.

And the answer is certainly not just 'accumulate more money'. Money is a tool, it is not the answer, it is an enabler, not the result. I've had clients with all the money in the world and no idea of what to do with it. Literally all they could think to talk to me about was the disdain they felt that their friends at the local club were entitled to more benefits from the government. I almost had to staple my jaw to my face so it didn't drop off.

So that's why I place so much significance on firstly identifying what your idea of financial freedom is. First tell me what do you want out of life – then lets get there together.

We started this chapter with three separate financial freedom scenarios. The private jet individual is going to need over $1,000,000 of cashflow per year, the individual who only wanted to work 2 days a week may need $50,000 cashflow per year, and the free spirited nature lover is probably going to get by on around $10,000 per year. Now we will figure out how much it will cost you to achieve your idea of financial freedom.

	Item cost per fortnight	Amount
Standard of Living	Accommodation	$
	Groceries	$
	Dining out	$
	Entertainment	$
	Regular payments (gym, insurance, etc)	$
	Other loan repayments (credit card etc)	$
Total		$

This will give you your basic fortnightly living expenses that you have grown accustomed to. Now multiply that by 26 and you have your annual cost of living.

We now add in anything else you would like to spend while enjoying your financial freedom

	Item cost per year	Amount
Optional Extras	Travel	$
	Additional lifestyle goals	$
Total		$

This table is for the things that you would like to do but you don't have the time or money to achieve them right now. Do you want to travel to Italy and live in Tuscany for a month every year for example, or do you want to want to learn to paint? These additional costs are generally bigger amounts and represent annual costs.

Once you have your standard of living costs and your annual option extras costs, you will be able to calculate the cost of living the life you want. This is the amount we need to get into your pockets every year to reach your idea of financial freedom.

Because ultimately achieving financial freedom is knowing what you want out of life, identifying how much it will cost, and then organizing weekly inflows of money to meet those costs.

And how are we going to pay for all these expenses? Well if your idea of financial freedom involves still working then it's a pretty easy situation – earn enough income to pay for all your expenses. If however you belong in the camp that screams 'I want weekly income without working', then what you are looking for is passive income.

Passive income is money that is earned by you in a manner that does not require you to trade in your time. The most common and well known example of this is rental income. A passive income source will drop money into your bank account every week without you having to do additional work for it. I've seen some very creative ones over the years such as selling ebooks through email mailing lists, or more conventional ones such as creating a business and having other people work for you. No matter what the source of this income is, the main thing to focus on when it comes to passive income is that you personally do not have to trade your time in order to earn money.

And before you can begin to enjoy the benefits of a passive income stream, you first need to create wealth. Wealth creation begins from the day you save your very first dollar. In horrifically boring economical terms it is called 'foregoing present consumption', but who talks like that? It is the understanding that there will come a time in your life that you won't be working and on that day you will begin receiving an income from that amount. This is when growth becomes less of a priority and the phrase 'cash is king' has never been more important.

As the scope of this chapter is not large enough to examine every possible avenue of creating wealth, I will list three ways. Once you create your wealth, you invest it to produce passive income.

1 – Inheritance. By far the easiest way to get rich and I highly recommend it as a method for gaining riches. Imagine, you're born, over time you become sentient and it slowly dawns on you that everyone else doesn't enjoy the luxuries you enjoy. Frivolities are your main concern, and the desire to attain self actualization is the only excuse you need to embark on your own 3 year pilgrimage. Now the only problem with this strategy is that it is very dictated to you based on genetics... namely your parents. So unless your family is adorned with crowns and seated on thrones or invested a large sum of money with Apple 30 years ago, I'd suggest this is going be a stretch.

2 – Invest. As my journey into the world of financial world commenced, this was my early favorite option. Like all young investors new to the game I

believed I could outperform the market with my infallible research skills, and that it was just a matter of time until the dollars started dropping into my lap. And I was indiscriminate in my choice towards asset classes. Firstly it was property. I ate books on how to make money from property. I believed what I read about property always going up in value, and discovered that the only problem with this knowledge was that everyone with any kind of clout had figured that out 20 years prior, and I was on the back end of a boom in the mid 2000's with no where to go. Yes property can be a good investment, but as a former tax accountant, I've done more than my fair share of real estate 'investment' tax returns, and very few people make a lot of money from them. So then I turned to the exciting world of equities. Pre GFC days I was there taking big risks on speculative stocks, riding the ups and selling out with profit. With all the success I was having, it was a wake up call when in late 2007 and then into 2008 lost all of my profits. It was a hard lesson to learn that investing is very hard work and not many people can make enough money to build wealth and live from the earnings. The risks are too big and if it goes the wrong way while pursuing large gains, you lose everything.

3 – Build a business. This is it. This is the hard one. The far less sexy one. The one that is day in day out, being diligent when you don't want to, and taking managed risks when you can. It's picking a passion or at the very least something you're good at, and making a go of it. This is the way people build real wealth. The reason is, while you are creating for yourself an income, you are actually building up the value of your company. So for example you pay yourself a salary of $50,000 for the year, but the value of your company increases by $100,000, then you've actually made $150,000. And the best news is the tax treatment of the $100,000 is substantially better then your $50,000 income.

Obviously becoming an entrepreneur is my most preferred option of creating wealth, and if you would like to read up on more about this, I suggest Richard Branson's biography titled 'losing my virginity', or Tim Ferris' book 'the four hour work week'. But the main goals of being an entrepreneur is having a businesses that will not require you to spend every day in the office in order to earn income. And if you are able to achieve this, then as soon as you are making enough passive income from your business to reach your idea of financial freedom, then you have to question why are you interested in making more. Don't forget in the pursuit of passive income, the real goal is spending the money on what it is you want to do with your life.

Once you have created wealth for yourself, it is now time to protect it with a diversified portfolio and begin to draw a passive income from it.

The Australian Securities and Investments Commission (ASIC) gives the opinion that the average 'Balanced' investor will earn around 6% per year in returns. A 'Balanced' investor will have anywhere between 50%-70% invested in growth assets of equities and property, with the remainder in bonds and cash. So using this conservative 6% rate of return, if you as the investor were to draw a little less than that of 5% as an income, then it is a common held view that your money will be able to pay you an income for the rest of you life.

So for example if you were to require $50,000 per year as an income, then you would need $1,000,000 invested.

And unless you are a very successful young entrepreneur and sell your business while you are still young, there is a good chance the only time you will be in a position to own such a large amount of money to invest, is once you have reached retirement and amassed a large amount of money over time.

And retirement brings some great opportunities and some unfortunate realities, which once again brings me back to identifying what you want out of life. Because on one hand you have the prospect of never having to work again. The world is your oyster and you can do all the things you've spent your whole life wanting to do. On the other hand if you do not prepare yourself for retirement by identifying what you want out of life, you are stuck with the reality of not being able to turn up to work on Monday. This can leave some people with a massive hole of time to fill in their day without anything to do, wishing they could go back and see their friends at work.

I have seen it many times, and once again it has nothing to do with the amount of money sitting in your retirement account, but it has everything to do with what your plans were for retirement. Not rocket science I know, but you will get what you want out of life. Plan – you will achieve your plans with the passive income earned, fail to plan and you will fall into the category of people who simply 'grow old'.

So as I mentioned before while investing is a difficult way to create wealth, it is the best way to protect wealth. And a well diversified portfolio with exposure to a combination of equities, property, bonds and cash has historically been a great way to keep your returns above the inflation rate while keeping volatility to a minimum.

Here is a basic overview of those 4 main asset classes. The percentage of each asset class you should aim for as an individual investor will depend on how aggressive you are, how much attention you pay to the market, whether you have a professional asset manager working for you, and how much time you have until retirement.

1 – Equities. Represents you owning a small portion of a publicly listed company. You share in any income the company earns, however the value of the asset you own will rise and fall every day, and sometimes those rises and falls are quite substantial. You will experience gains and losses every day, and that's why it is good practice to own a portfolio of shares. As on any given day, a fall in a equity will be offset by a gain in another, and as these

companies grow, the value of your asset should grow also over time. Unless you spend a substantial amount of time researching the market, reading balance sheets, meeting with the management team, and completing your own research on a monthly basis for each company you own, I would question whether or not you should outsource this research to fund managers.

Fund managers spend all day every day researching the equities they invest your money for, and in my experience have outperformed my personal investment choices every year for the last decade. It is now my personal preference to invest my money into small boutique fund managers who own the companies they invest for. My reasoning is, generally they are the best of the best.

These men and women will start their career choosing stocks for big well established companies, until their method consistently outperforms the market, then they decide to leave the big corporate investment fund and continue with their investment mandates but with less red tape in their own boutique investment fund. Then you watch and wait a few years to see if their new investment management team performs well, and if the team is once again outperforming the market, then it's time to sit down and consider letting them invest some of your money. A financial adviser like myself can help you choose which investment teams have this background and consistent investment returns.

2 – Property. Is considered the second 'growth' asset and is also volatile with great historical returns. The only difference is that property is valued not valued on a daily basis, and therefore experiences less volatility. This is often people's favourite investment option as it is 'bricks and mortar', and the investor can drive past the house and 'see' their investments. In a well diversified portfolio, property will make up a portion of the total overall investments, however I do see investors overweight in property quite a bit.

I understand why, it has been a great investment over the last 20 years especially here in Australia, however the reasons for that growth are often disputed, and whether or not it can continue is a point that should not be ignored.

3 – Bonds. Bonds are probably the least well understood asset class. To think of it simply, in the same way that you borrow money from the bank to purchase a house and in return pay back the initial amount you borrowed plus interest, well when you purchase a bond you are lending money to a company or government in return to be paid back plus an amount of interest. Bonds are considered a 'defensive' asset, however there is volatility involved so the investment is not as safe as money in the bank.

4 – Cash. Is simply just in the bank. Both money invested in term deposits which lock your money in for a set amount of time, and money just sitting in the bank. Both are considered the safest option of investing and requires very little investment understanding to get started. Give your money to the bank, and they will keep it and give you a little extra. It is still a valuable part of a diversified portfolio as it gives some stability during volatile times.

Finally after this brief overview of how to pay for what you want out of life, lets finish this with the most important part again - achieving your idea of financial freedom. As I deal with this on a day to day basis, I want to emphasise that it is different for everyone, and you should spend the most time on what you want out of life.

There are a lot of flashing lights out there and shiny things to own, so make sure you pursue what it is you want. And if you have never sat down and thought about it, now is a great time to start. Know that you deserve all the happiness in the world, and if you plan it early enough you can have everything you want.

So if you're young start now. If you're about to retire, then there are a few things that you can do now that will greatly increase your success even at this late stage, and if you're already retired I hope you had a chance to hear to this kind of advice when you did something about it. All the best to your financial freedom.

Clayton Daniel

About the author

Enjoy today. Relax tomorrow.

These four words define the meaning of why I am a financial adviser. For too long I have seen people either eagerly throw away today in order to benefit tomorrow, or be too caught up in the moment to ever think of their future. I consider myself the peace broker of both. If you have spent your entire life at work, it's probably time for a holiday. If you have just arrived home from your sixth around the world trip, then let's talk about what tomorrow looks like. Starting out as a tax accountant and moving on to para-planning for Self Managed Super Funds, one of my key strengths is my knowledge of Australian taxation and superannuation law. I am now the director of Hillross Silverstone, a boutique financial advice firm aimed at long term strategic financial advice specifically for affluent and active people. Designed to maximise, consolidate and simplify your financial life.